PHILIP'S JUNIOR SCHOOL ATLAS

Philip's is proud to announce that its World Atlases are now published in association with The Royal Geographical Society (with The Institute of British Geographers).

The Society was founded in 1830 and given a Royal Charter in 1859 for 'the advancement of geographical science'. Today it is a leading world centre for geographical learning – supporting education, teaching, research and expeditions, and promoting public understanding of the subject.

Further information about the Society and how to join may be found on its website at: www.rgs.org

Published in Great Britain by George Philip Limited, a division of Octopus Publishing Group Limited, 2–4 Heron Quays, London E14 4JP

in association with Reed Primary, Halley Court, Jordan Hill, Oxford OX2 8EJ

Cartography by Philip's

Page 2 Bath city map (top right) – Based upon the Ordnance Survey mapping with the permission of The Controller of Her Majesty's Stationery Office © Crown Copyright 399817

Illustrations by Stefan Chabluk

© 1993, 1999 George Philip Limited
First published 1993
Second edition 1997
Third edition 1999
Reprinted 2000

A CIP catalogue record for this book is available from the British Library.

ISBN 0–540–07698–8

Printed in China

Details of other Philip's titles and services can be found on our website at: www.philips-maps.co.uk

What is a map?

These small maps explain the meaning of some of the lines and colours on the atlas maps.

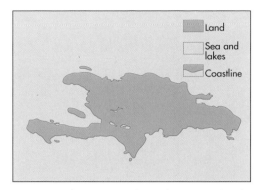

1. Land and sea This is how an island is shown on a map. The land is coloured green and the sea is blue. The coastline is a blue line.

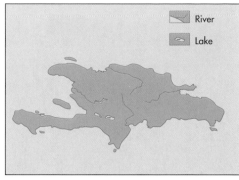

2. Rivers and lakes There are some lakes on the island and rivers that flow down to the sea.

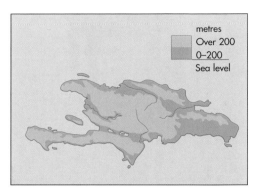

3. Height of the land – 1 This map shows the land over 200 metres high in a lighter colour. The height of the land is shown by contour lines and layer colours.

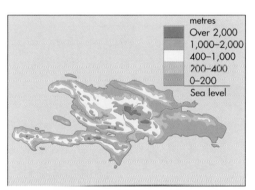

4. Height of the land – 2 This map shows more contour lines and layer colours. It shows that the highest land is in the centre of the island and that it is over 2,000 metres high.

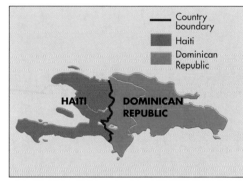

5. Countries This is a way of showing different information about the island. It shows that the island is divided into two countries. They are separated by a country boundary.

6. Cities and towns There are cities and towns on the island. The two capital cities are shown with a special symbol. Other large or important cities are also shown by a red square or circle.

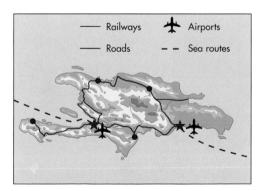

7. Transport information This map shows the most important roads, railways, airports and sea routes. Transport routes connect the cities and towns.

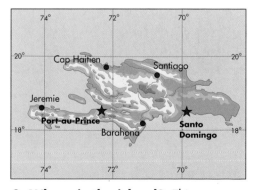

8. Where is the island? This map gives the lines of latitude and longitude and shows where the island is in the world. Page 59 in the atlas shows the same island at a different scale.

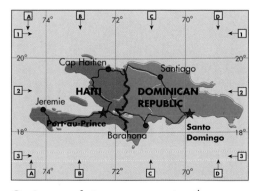

9. A complete map – using the country colouring and showing the letter-figure codes used in the index.

Scale

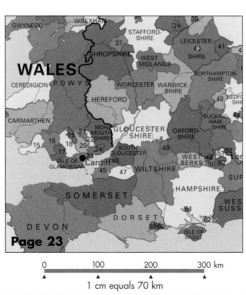

1 cm equals 200 m

This is a drawing of the top of a table, looking down on it. It is 100 cm wide and 50 cm from front to back. The drawing measures 4 × 2 cm. It is drawn to scale: 1 cm on the drawing equals 25 cm on the table.

This is a plan of a room looking down from above. 1 cm on the map equals 1 metre in the room. The same table is shown, but now at a smaller scale. Use the scale bar to find the measurements of other parts of the room.

This is a map of an area in the city of Bath. Large buildings can be seen but other buildings are too small to show. Below are atlas maps of different scales.

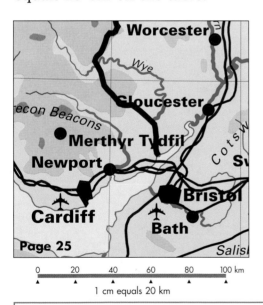

Page 25

1 cm equals 20 km

Page 23

1 cm equals 70 km

Page 50

1 cm equals 150 km

Scale bars
This distance represents 1 mile

This distance represents 1 kilometre

These examples of scale bars are at the scale of 1 cm equals 0.5 km

Signposts still have miles on them. 1 mile = 1.6 km, or 10 miles is the same as 16 kilometres. On maps of continents in this atlas, both a kilometre and a mile scale bar are shown.

On the maps of the continents, where you cannot see the British Isles, a small map of the British Isles is shown. It gives you some idea of size and scale.

BRITISH ISLES
On same scale

Direction

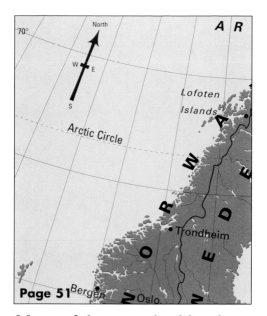

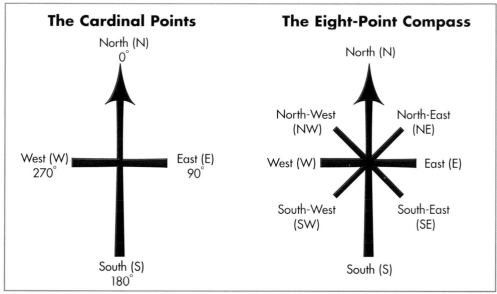

Many of the maps in this atlas have a North Point showing the direction of north. It points in the same direction as the lines of longitude. The four main directions shown are called the cardinal points.

Direction is measured in degrees. This diagram shows the degree numbers for each cardinal point. The direction is measured clockwise from north. The diagram on the right shows all the points of the compass and the divisions between the cardinal points. For example, between north and east there is north-east, between south and west is south-west. You can work out the cardinal points at your home by looking for the sun rising in the east and setting in the west.

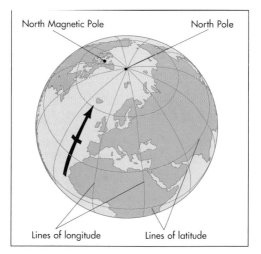

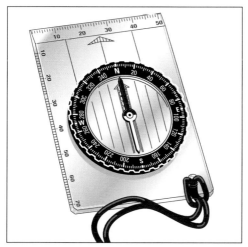

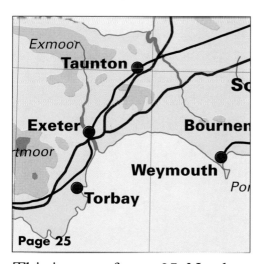

The Earth has a spot near the North Pole that is called the Magnetic Pole. If a piece of metal that was magnetized at one end was left to float, then the magnetized tip would point to the North Magnetic Pole.

The needle of a compass is magnetized and it always points north. If you know where you are and want to go to another place, you can measure your direction from a map and use a compass to guide you.

This is part of map 25. North is at the top. Look at the points of the compass on the diagram above and the positions of places on the map. Taunton is north-east of Exeter and Weymouth is south-east of Taunton.

Latitude and longitude

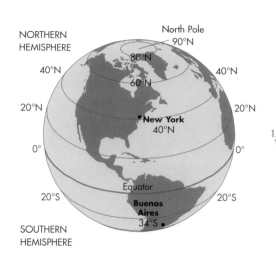

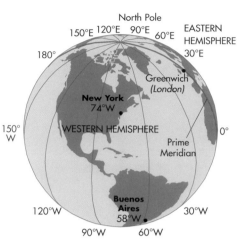

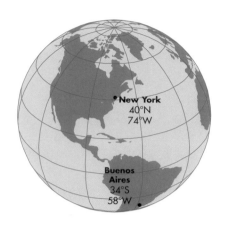

Latitude

This map shows how the Earth would look from thousands of kilometres above New York. The Equator is exactly halfway between the North and South Poles. It divides the Earth into two hemispheres. The Equator is shown as a line on maps. It is numbered 0°. There are other lines on maps north and south of the Equator. They are called lines of latitude.

Longitude

Maps have another set of lines running north to south linking the Poles. These lines are called lines of longitude. The line numbered 0° runs through Greenwich in London, England, and is called the Prime Meridian. The other lines of longitude are numbered up to 180° east and west of 0°. Longitude line 180° runs through the Pacific Ocean.

Map references

The latitude and longitude lines on maps form a grid. In this atlas, the grid lines are in blue, and on most maps are shown for every ten degrees. The numbers of the lines can be used to give a reference to show the location of a place on a map. The index in this atlas uses another way of finding places. It lists the rows of latitude as numbers and the columns of longitude as letters.

Line of latitude with its number in degrees

Line of longitude with its number in degrees

Row number used in the index

Column letter used in the index

This table shows the largest city in each continent with its latitude and longitude. Look for them on the maps in this atlas.

	Latitude	Longitude	Map page	Map letter-figure
Cairo	30°N	31°E	55	F2
Mexico City	19°N	99°W	59	H7
Moscow	56°N	38°E	51	Q4
Sao Paulo	24°S	48°W	61	F6
Shanghai	31°N	121°E	53	P5
Sydney	34°N	151°E	57	F11

Map information

Symbols

A map symbol shows the position of something – for example, circles for towns or an aeroplane for an airport.

▼

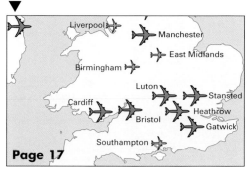

Page 17

On some maps a dot or a symbol stands for a large number for example, ten million people or two million tonnes of wheat or potatoes.

▼

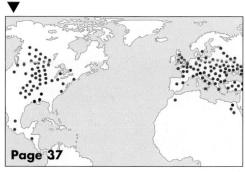

Page 37

The size of the symbol can be bigger or smaller, to show different numbers. The symbol here shows tourists.

▼

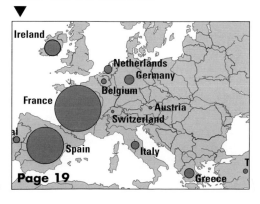

Page 19

Colours

1. Colours are used on some maps so that separate areas, such as countries, as in this map, can be seen clearly.

▼

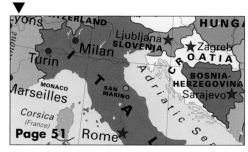

Page 51

3. Patterns on maps often spread across country borders. This map shows different types of vegetation in the world.

▼

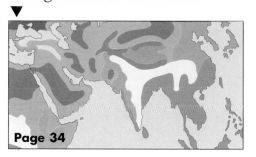

Page 34

2. On other maps, areas which are the same in some way have the same colour to show patterns. This map shows rainfall.

▼

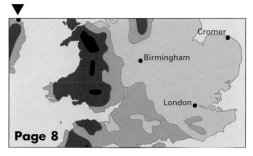

Page 8

4. Colours that are lighter or darker are used on some maps to show less or more of something. This map shows farming.

▼

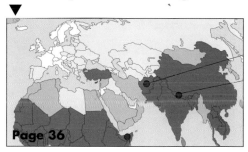

Page 36

Graphs and charts

Graphs and charts are used to give more information about subjects shown on the maps. A graph shows how something changes over time.

This graph shows the rainfall for each month in a year as a blue bar which can be measured on the scale at the side of the graph.

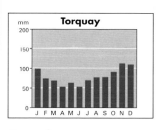

Page 8

This diagram is called a pie-chart. It shows how you can divide a total into its parts.

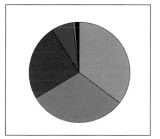

Page 15

This is a bar-chart. It is another way of showing a total divided into parts.

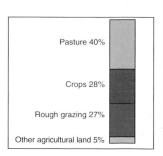

Pasture 40%

Crops 28%

Rough grazing 27%

Other agricultural land 5%

Page 13

— Rocks, mountains and rivers—

Rocks

This map shows the different types of rock in Great Britain and Ireland.

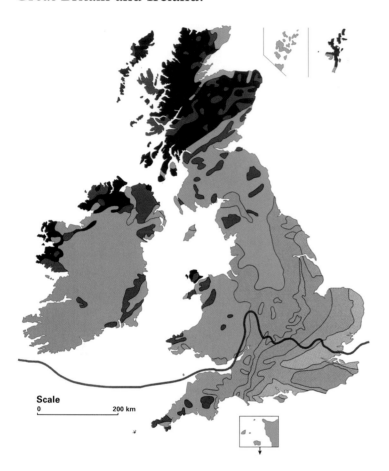

Scale

0   200 km

Type of rock

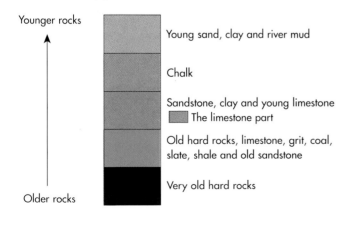

Younger rocks ↑

Young sand, clay and river mud

Chalk

Sandstone, clay and young limestone
☐ The limestone part

Old hard rocks, limestone, grit, coal, slate, shale and old sandstone

Very old hard rocks

Older rocks

Old volcanoes, granite and basalt

Glaciers came as far south as this line up to 10,000 years ago

Longest rivers		Largest islands	
(length in kilometres)		(square kilometres)	
Shannon	370	Great Britain	229,880
Severn	354	Ireland	84,400
Thames	335	Lewis and Harris	2,225
Trent	297	Skye	1,666
Aire	259	Shetland (Mainland)	967
Ouse	230	Mull	899
Wye	215	Anglesey	714
Tay	188	Islay	615
Nene	161	Isle of Man	572
Clyde	158	Isle of Wight	381

Largest lakes

(square kilometres)

Lough Neagh	382
Lough Corrib	168
Lough Derg	120
Lower Lough Erne	105
Loch Lomond	71
Loch Ness	57

The largest lake in England is Lake Windermere (15 square kilometres). The largest lake in Wales is Lake Vyrnwy (8 square kilometres).

Highest mountains

(height in metres)

In Scotland:
  Ben Nevis 1,347
In Wales:
  Snowdon 1,085
In Ireland:
  Carrauntoohill 1,041
In England:
  Scafell Pike 978
In Northern Ireland:
  Slieve Donard 852

Scale

0   200 km

6

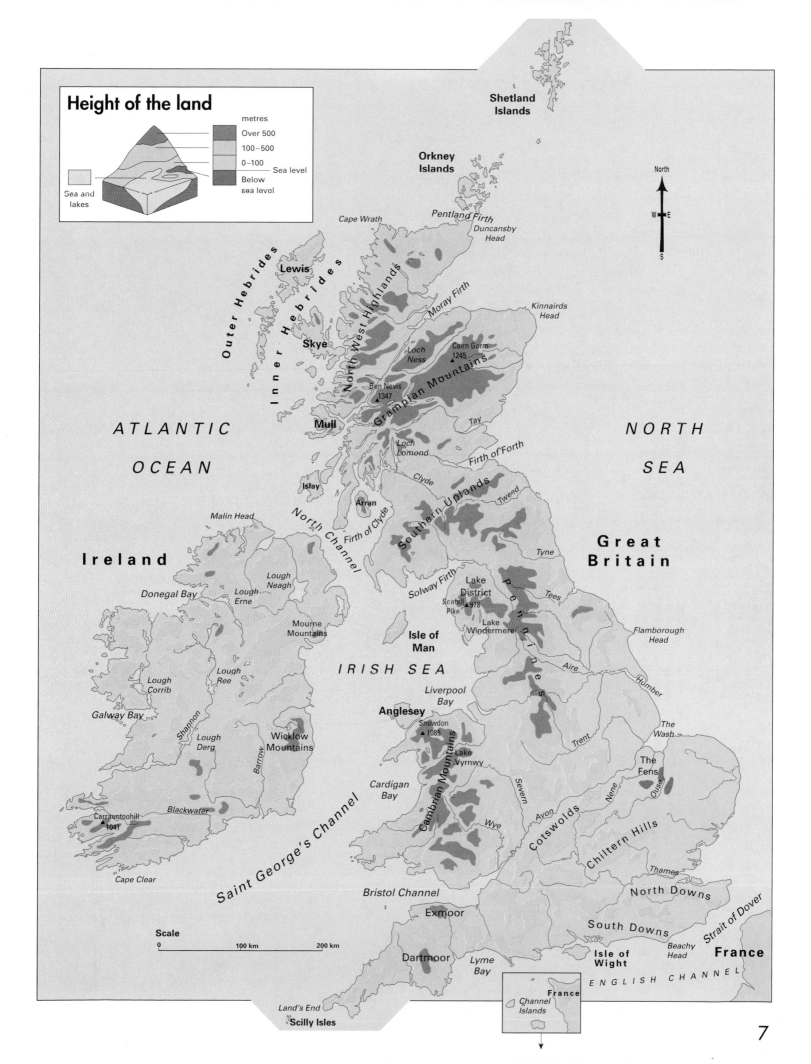

Height of the land

metres
Over 500
100–500
0–100
Sea level
Below sea level

Sea and lakes

Shetland Islands

Orkney Islands

Pentland Firth

Cape Wrath

Duncansby Head

North

W E

S

Lewis

Outer Hebrides

Inner Hebrides

Skye

North West Highlands

Moray Firth

Kinnairds Head

Loch Ness

Cairn Gorm 1245

Grampian Mountains

Ben Nevis 1347

Mull

Tay

Loch Lomond

Islay

Arran

Firth of Clyde

Clyde

Firth of Forth

Southern Uplands

Tweed

N O R T H

S E A

A T L A N T I C

O C E A N

Malin Head

North Channel

Ireland

Donegal Bay

Lough Erne

Lough Neagh

Tyne

Great Britain

Solway Firth

Lake District

Scafell Pike 978

Pennines

Tees

Flamborough Head

Mourne Mountains

Lake Windermere

Isle of Man

Lough Corrib

Lough Ree

Lough Derg

I R I S H   S E A

Aire

Humber

Liverpool Bay

Anglesey

Galway Bay

Shannon

Barrow

Wicklow Mountains

Snowdon 1085

Lake Vyrnwy

Cambrian Mountains

Trent

The Wash

Carrauntoohill 1041

Blackwater

Cardigan Bay

The Fens

Nene

Ouse

Saint George's Channel

Severn

Wye

Avon

Cotswolds

Chiltern Hills

Cape Clear

Bristol Channel

Exmoor

North Downs

Thames

South Downs

Strait of Dover

Land's End

Scilly Isles

Dartmoor

Lyme Bay

Isle of Wight

Beachy Head

France

E N G L I S H   C H A N N E L

France
Channel Islands

Scale
0   100 km   200 km

Rainfall is measured at many places in the UK every day. Each year, all the measurements are put together and graphs are made, like the ones shown on this page. Experts in the weather use these measurements to find out the average amount of rainfall in the UK for each year. They can then show this on weather maps, like the map below. Graphs and maps are also made for average temperatures and other types of weather (see opposite page). These help the experts to see patterns in the UK's weather over a long period of time. These patterns in the weather show a country's climate. The maps on these pages show you the climate of the UK.

If you collect the rainfall each day and measure it, then you could draw a graph like this.

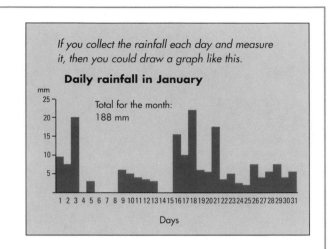

Daily rainfall in January

Total for the month: 188 mm

Rainfall

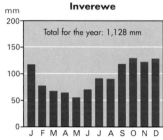

Inverewe
Total for the year: 1,128 mm

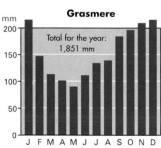

Grasmere
Total for the year: 1,851 mm

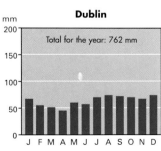

Dublin
Total for the year: 762 mm

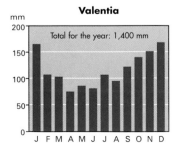

Valentia
Total for the year: 1,400 mm

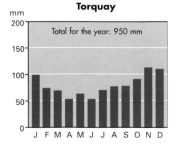

Torquay
Total for the year: 950 mm

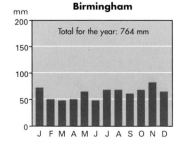

Birmingham
Total for the year: 764 mm

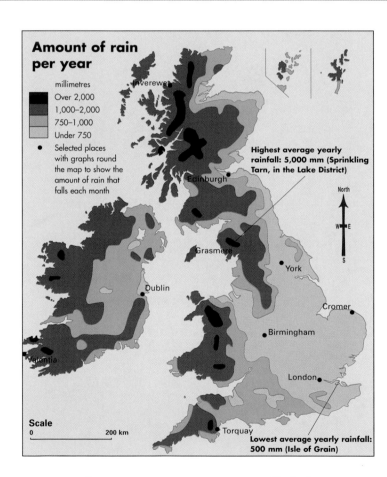

Amount of rain per year

millimetres
Over 2,000
1,000–2,000
750–1,000
Under 750
• Selected places with graphs round the map to show the amount of rain that falls each month

Highest average yearly rainfall: 5,000 mm (Sprinkling Tarn, in the Lake District)

Lowest average yearly rainfall: 500 mm (Isle of Grain)

Scale
0   200 km

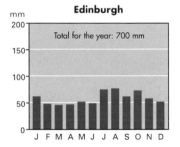

Edinburgh
Total for the year: 700 mm

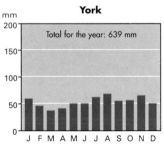

York
Total for the year: 639 mm

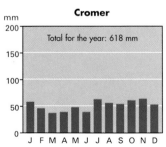

Cromer
Total for the year: 618 mm

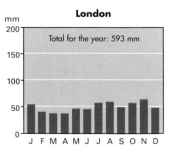

London
Total for the year: 593 mm

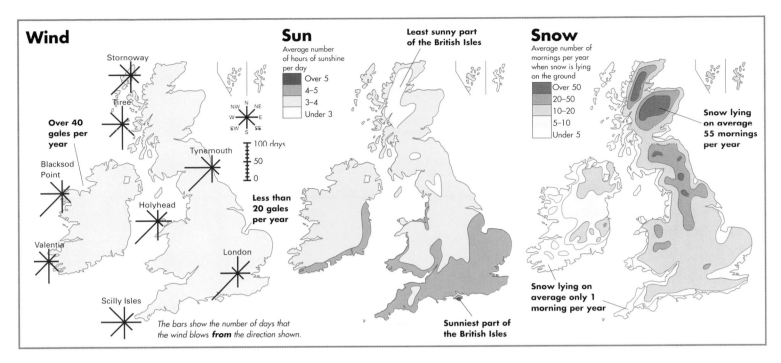

Wind

Stornoway
Tiree

Over 40 gales per year

Blacksod Point

Less than 20 gales per year

Tynemouth

Holyhead

Valentia

London

Scilly Isles

*The bars show the number of days that the wind blows **from** the direction shown.*

Sun

Average number of hours of sunshine per day

	Over 5
	4–5
	3–4
	Under 3

100 days
50
0

Least sunny part of the British Isles

Sunniest part of the British Isles

Snow

Average number of mornings per year when snow is lying on the ground

	Over 50
	20–50
	10–20
	5–10
	Under 5

Snow lying on average 55 mornings per year

Snow lying on average only 1 morning per year

Temperature

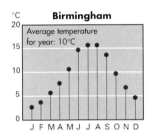

Birmingham
°C
20
Average temperature for year: 10°C
15
10
5
0
J F M A M J J A S O N D

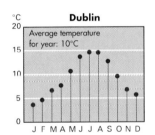

Dublin
°C
20
Average temperature for year: 10°C
15
10
5
0
J F M A M J J A S O N D

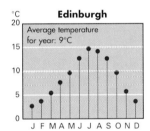

Edinburgh
°C
20
Average temperature for year: 9°C
15
10
5
0
J F M A M J J A S O N D

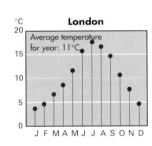

London
°C
20
Average temperature for year: 11°C
15
10
5
0
J F M A M J J A S O N D

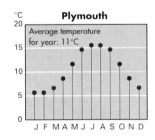

Plymouth
°C
20
Average temperature for year: 11°C
15
10
5
0
J F M A M J J A S O N D

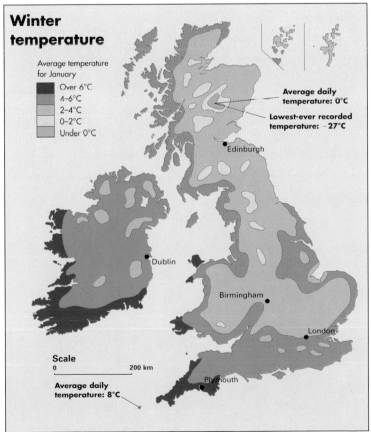

Winter temperature

Average temperature for January

	Over 6°C
	4–6°C
	2–4°C
	0–2°C
	Under 0°C

Average daily temperature: 0°C

Lowest-ever recorded temperature: −27°C

Edinburgh

Dublin

Birmingham

London

Scale
0   200 km

Average daily temperature: 8°C

Plymouth

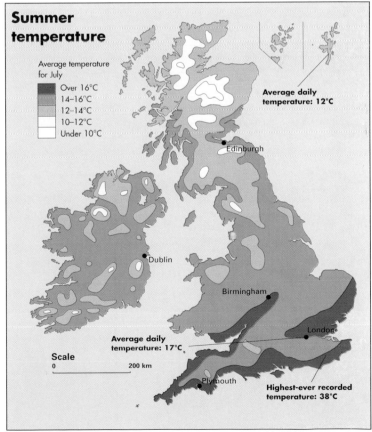

Summer temperature

Average temperature for July

	Over 16°C
	14–16°C
	12–14°C
	10–12°C
	Under 10°C

Average daily temperature: 12°C

Edinburgh

Dublin

Birmingham

Average daily temperature: 17°C

London

Scale
0   200 km

Plymouth

Highest-ever recorded temperature: 38°C

9

People, cities and towns

The Census

Every ten years, there is a government survey in the UK. The head of each household has to fill in a form. On the form, there are questions about the house and the people who live there. This is called the Census. The Census tells the government the number of people living in the UK. This helps the government plan such things as schools and hospitals. The Census shows how the population has changed from the beginning of the century to the early 1990s.

Here are some of the questions asked on the Census form:

Age?
Have you moved house in the last year?
In which country were you born?
To which ethnic group do you belong?
Have you a long-term illness?
Can you speak Welsh?
What do you do for a job?
How many hours a week do you work?
How do you get to work?
Where do you work?
Do you own or rent your house?
Do you have a bath, flush toilet or central heating?
Do you have a car?

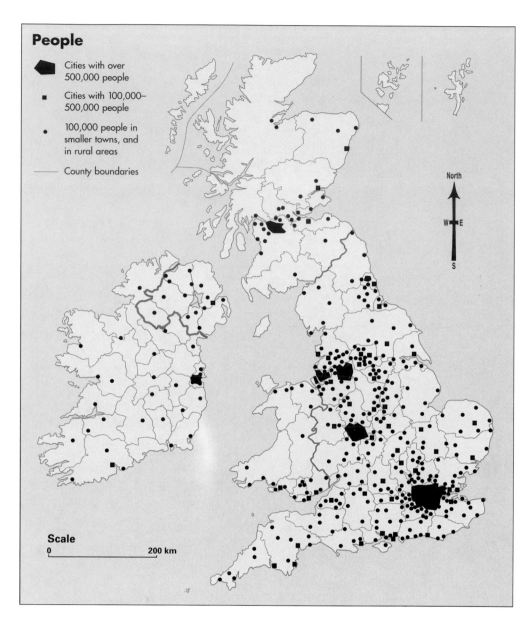

People

- Cities with over 500,000 people
- Cities with 100,000–500,000 people
- 100,000 people in smaller towns, and in rural areas
- County boundaries

North
W E
S

Scale
0 _____ 200 km

Country population data

	1901	1951	1991
		millions	
England	30.5	41.2	48.1
Wales	2.0	2.6	2.9
Scotland	4.5	5.1	5.1
Northern Ireland	1.2	1.4	1.6
United Kingdom	**38.2**	**50.3**	**57.6**
Isle of Man	0.055	0.005	0.062
Channel Islands	0.096	0.102	0.139
Ireland	**3.2**	**2.9**	**3.5**

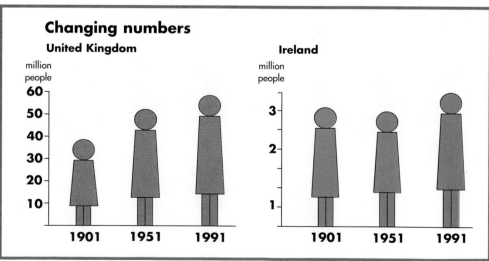

Changing numbers

United Kingdom

million people

60
50
40
30
20
10

1901 1951 1991

Ireland

million people

3

2

1

1901 1951 1991

Cities

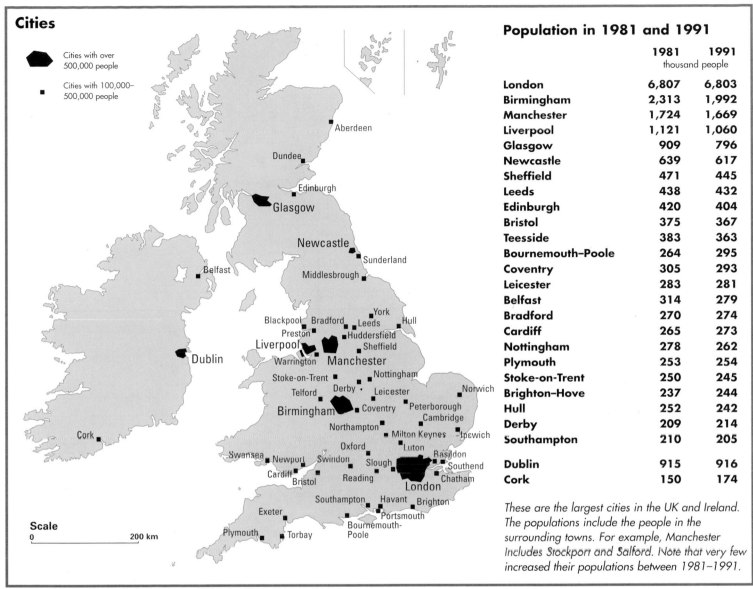

Cities with over 500,000 people

■ Cities with 100,000–500,000 people

Scale
0 ——————— 200 km

Population in 1981 and 1991

	1981	1991
	thousand people	
London	6,807	6,803
Birmingham	2,313	1,992
Manchester	1,724	1,669
Liverpool	1,121	1,060
Glasgow	909	796
Newcastle	639	617
Sheffield	471	445
Leeds	438	432
Edinburgh	420	404
Bristol	375	367
Teesside	383	363
Bournemouth–Poole	264	295
Coventry	305	293
Leicester	283	281
Belfast	314	279
Bradford	270	274
Cardiff	265	273
Nottingham	278	262
Plymouth	253	254
Stoke-on-Trent	250	245
Brighton–Hove	237	244
Hull	252	242
Derby	209	214
Southampton	210	205
Dublin	915	916
Cork	150	174

These are the largest cities in the UK and Ireland. The populations include the people in the surrounding towns. For example, Manchester includes Stockport and Salford. Note that very few increased their populations between 1981–1991.

Young people

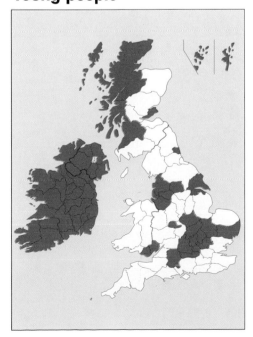

In these counties, young people are a large group in the population (over about 20%). On this map young people are those aged under 15 years old.

In these counties, old people are a large group in the population (over 20%). On this map old people are women aged over 60 and men over 65 years old.

Look at these two maps. Can you think of some reasons why some counties have more older people than other counties?

Old people

Farming and fishing

Types of farm

Dairy farms
Cows for milk, butter and cheese

Beef farms
Cows and calves for beef and veal

Sheep farms
Sheep and lambs for wool and meat

Grain and root farms
Wheat, potatoes, sugar beet and oilseed rape

Mixed farms
Livestock and grain or roots

Market gardening
Vegetables, fruit and flowers

Forests

Big cities

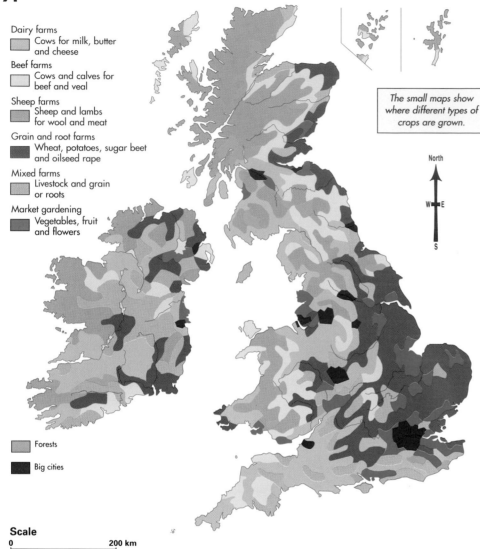

The small maps show where different types of crops are grown.

North
W — E
S

Scale
0 _____ 200 km

Wheat

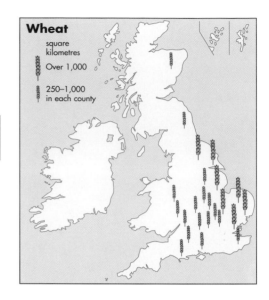

square kilometres

Over 1,000

250–1,000 in each county

Potatoes

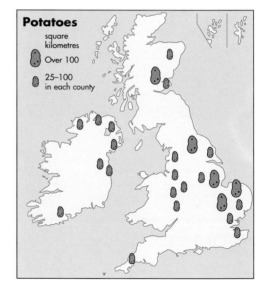

square kilometres

Over 100

25–100 in each county

Oilseed rape

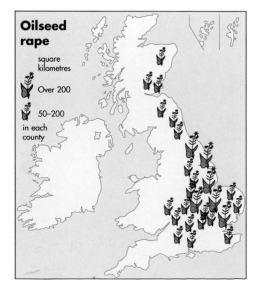

square kilometres

Over 200

50–200 in each county

Sugar beet

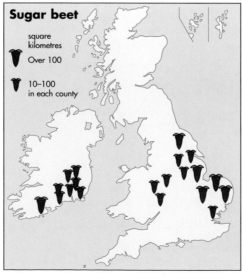

square kilometres

Over 100

10–100 in each county

Vegetables

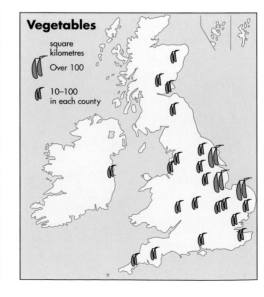

square kilometres

Over 100

10–100 in each county

12

Cattle

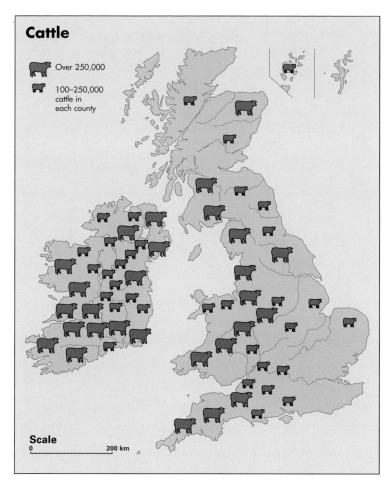

Over 250,000

100–250,000 cattle in each county

Scale

0   200 km

Sheep and pigs

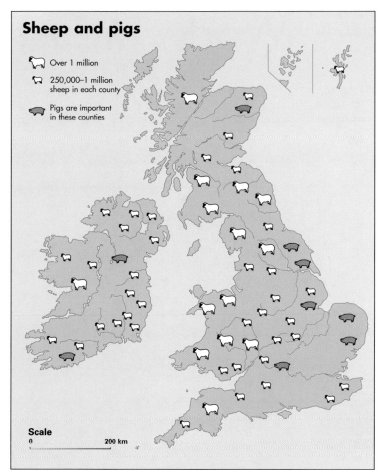

Over 1 million

250,000–1 million sheep in each county

Pigs are important in these counties

Scale

0   200 km

Land use in the UK

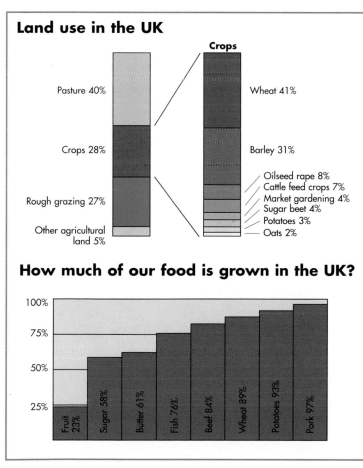

Crops

Pasture 40%

Crops 28%

Rough grazing 27%

Other agricultural land 5%

Wheat 41%

Barley 31%

Oilseed rape 8%
Cattle feed crops 7%
Market gardening 4%
Sugar beet 4%
Potatoes 3%
Oats 2%

How much of our food is grown in the UK?

Fruit 23%
Sugar 58%
Butter 61%
Fish 76%
Beef 84%
Wheat 89%
Potatoes 93%
Pork 97%

Fishing

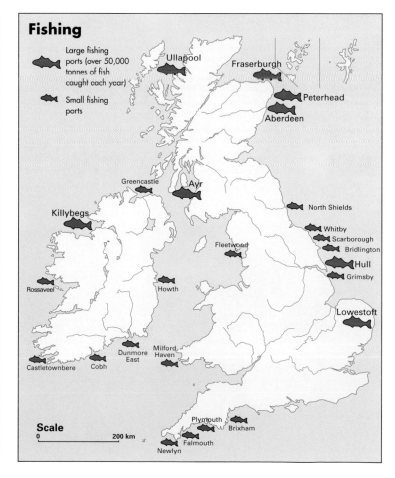

Large fishing ports (over 50,000 tonnes of fish caught each year)

Small fishing ports

Ullapool
Fraserburgh
Peterhead
Aberdeen
Greencastle
Ayr
North Shields
Killybegs
Whitby
Scarborough
Bridlington
Fleetwood
Hull
Grimsby
Rossaveel
Howth
Lowestoft
Castletownbere
Cobh
Dunmore East
Milford Haven
Plymouth
Brixham
Falmouth
Newlyn

Scale

0   200 km

— Work, industry and energy —

Manufacturing

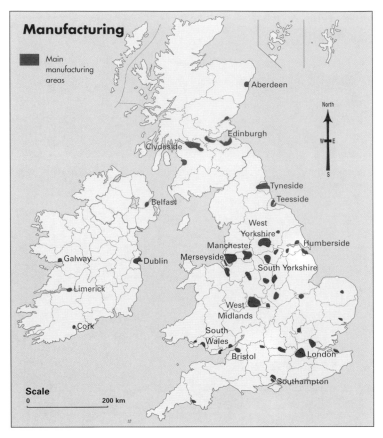

Main manufacturing areas

Aberdeen

Edinburgh

Clydeside

Tyneside
Teesside

Belfast

West Yorkshire
Manchester
Merseyside
South Yorkshire
Humberside

Galway
Dublin

Limerick

Cork

West Midlands

South Wales

Bristol
London

Southampton

North

Scale
0   200 km

Manufacturing industries are industries which make things. Some examples of manufactured goods are cars, steel, textiles and clothes.

Unemployment

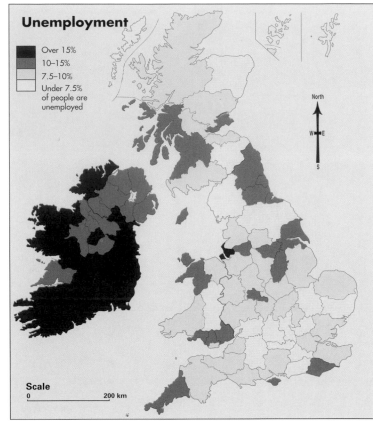

- Over 15%
- 10–15%
- 7.5–10%
- Under 7.5% of people are unemployed

North

Scale
0   200 km

Service industries do not make things. They provide a service to people. Shops, hotels and banks are examples of service industries.

Employment in manufacturing

Over 25% of people who work are employed in manufacturing industries

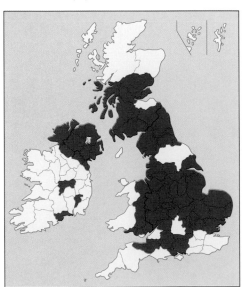

Employment in services

Over 70% of people who work are employed in the service industries

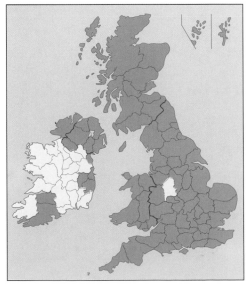

Employment in agriculture

% of people who work are employed in agriculture, forestry or fishing

Over 10%   2.5–10%

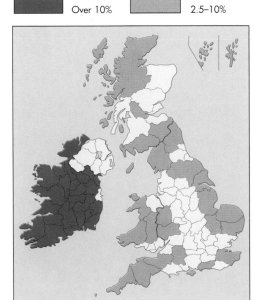

Sources of energy used in the United Kingdom

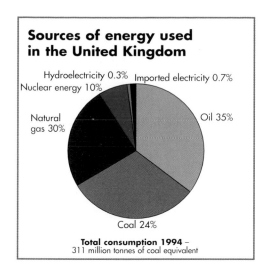

Hydroelectricity 0.3%
Imported electricity 0.7%
Nuclear energy 10%
Natural gas 30%
Oil 35%
Coal 24%

Total consumption 1994 –
311 million tonnes of coal equivalent

Types of energy production, 1960–1990

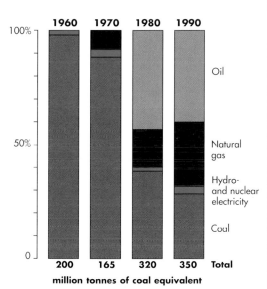

100%

50%

0

1960	1970	1980	1990	

Oil

Natural gas

Hydro- and nuclear electricity

Coal

200	165	320	350	**Total**

million tonnes of coal equivalent

This is the energy produced in the UK and from the sea around the UK. Some of this is exported and some energy sources are imported. The totals are given in million tonnes of coal. This means that all the figures have been turned into the energy they would make if they were coal.

Coal mining and miners in the UK, 1950–1994

	1950	1970	1994
Number of miners (in thousands)	686	356	10
Number of mines	901	292	54
Coal produced (million tonnes)	220	145	53

You can see from the table that there were less mines and miners in 1994 than 1950. Britain's pits and open-cast mines were sold by the government on 30 December 1994 (ending 48 years of state ownership). The new owners paid almost £1,000 million to the government for the mines and coal reserves. There are thought to be 700 million tonnes of coal left in the ground.

Energy sources in Great Britain and Ireland

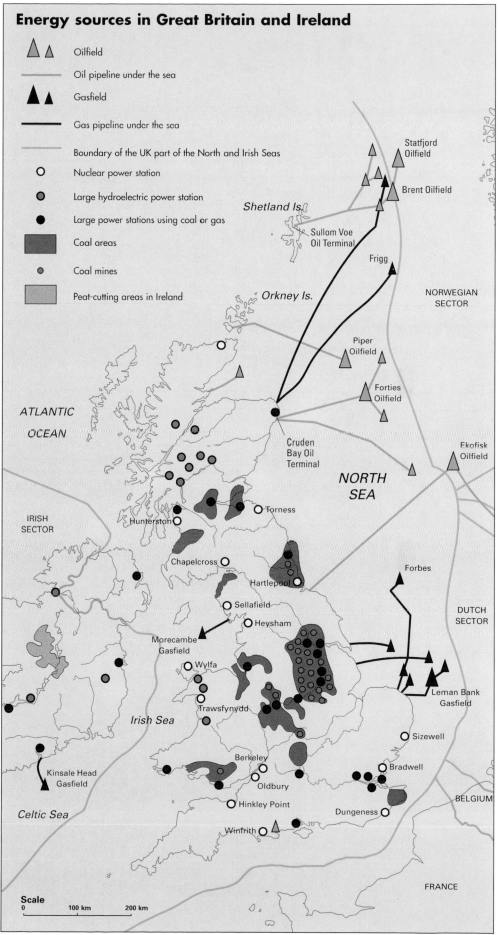

- Oilfield
- Oil pipeline under the sea
- Gasfield
- Gas pipeline under the sea
- Boundary of the UK part of the North and Irish Seas
- Nuclear power station
- Large hydroelectric power station
- Large power stations using coal or gas
- Coal areas
- Coal mines
- Peat-cutting areas in Ireland

Statfjord Oilfield
Brent Oilfield
Shetland Is.
Sullom Voe Oil Terminal
Frigg
Orkney Is.
NORWEGIAN SECTOR
Piper Oilfield
Forties Oilfield
ATLANTIC OCEAN
Cruden Bay Oil Terminal
Ekofisk Oilfield
NORTH SEA
IRISH SECTOR
Torness
Hunterston
Chapelcross
Hartlepool
Forbes
Sellafield
Heysham
DUTCH SECTOR
Morecambe Gasfield
Wylfa
Trawsfynydd
Irish Sea
Leman Bank Gasfield
Sizewell
Kinsale Head Gasfield
Berkeley
Bradwell
Oldbury
Hinkley Point
Dungeness
BELGIUM
Celtic Sea
Winfrith
FRANCE

Scale
0   100 km   200 km

15

Transport

There are about 370 thousand kilometres of road in the UK. The total number of cars, buses, lorries and motorbikes is 25 million. That is almost half the number of people in the UK. The maps on this page show the motorways and some main roads in the UK and the number of cars in the different regions. At the bottom of the page there are tables showing the road distances between important towns.

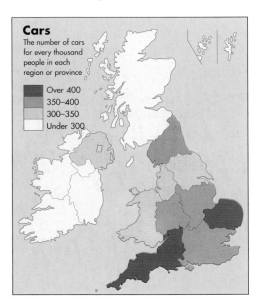

Cars

The number of cars for every thousand people in each region or province

- Over 400
- 350–400
- 300–350
- Under 300

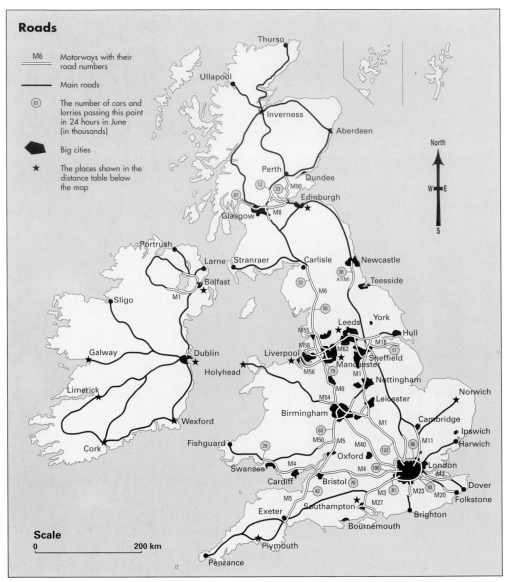

Roads

M6	Motorways with their road numbers
	Main roads
67	The number of cars and lorries passing this point in 24 hours in June (in thousands)
	Big cities
★	The places shown in the distance table below the map

Scale

0   200 km

North
W — E
S

UK	Birmingham	Cardiff	Edinburgh	Holyhead	Inverness	Leeds	Liverpool	London	Manchester	Norwich	Plymouth	Southampton
Birmingham		163	460	246	716	179	151	179	130	249	320	206
Cardiff	163		587	341	843	341	264	249	277	381	259	192
Edinburgh	460	587		489	256	320	338	608	336	586	790	669
Holyhead	246	341	489		745	262	151	420	198	481	528	455
Inverness	716	843	256	745		579	605	864	604	842	1049	925
Leeds	179	341	320	262	579		119	306	64	277	502	378
Liverpool	151	264	338	151	605	119		330	55	360	452	357
London	179	249	608	420	864	306	330		309	172	343	127
Manchester	130	277	336	198	604	64	55	309		306	457	325
Norwich	249	381	586	481	842	277	360	172	306		515	299
Plymouth	320	259	790	528	1049	·502	452	343	457	515		246
Southampton	206	192	669	455	925	378	357	127	325	299	246	

Road distances

The distance tables are in kilometres, but distances on road signposts in the UK are in miles.
A mile is longer than a kilometre.
1 mile = 1.6 kilometres. 1 kilometre = 0.6 mile.

Ireland

	Belfast	Cork	Dublin	Galway	Limerick	Wexford
Belfast		418	160	300	222	306
Cork	418		257	193	97	190
Dublin	160	257		210	193	137
Galway	300	193	210		97	249
Limerick	222	97	193	97		193
Wexford	306	190	137	249	193	

Railways

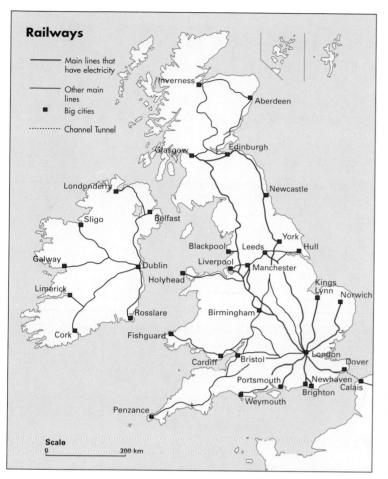

- Main lines that have electricity
- Other main lines
- ■ Big cities
- ⋯⋯ Channel Tunnel

Scale
0 ___ 200 km

Manchester – the daily flow of people

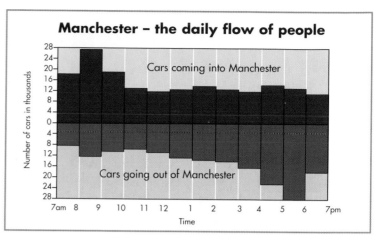

Number of cars in thousands

28 24 20 16 12 8 4 0 4 8 12 16 20 24 28

Cars coming into Manchester

Cars going out of Manchester

7am 8 9 10 11 12 1 2 3 4 5 6 7pm
Time

The Channel Tunnel

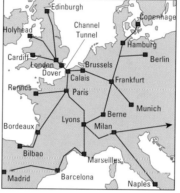

The Channel Tunnel is 50 kilometres long and trains run through it in just 21 minutes.

Journey time to Paris by train		
	hours and minutes	
from	Today	Year 2010
London	3.00	2.30
Birmingham	6.30	4.15
Manchester	8.15	5.15
Newcastle	8.30	6.00
Edinburgh	10.00	7.30

By the year 2010 trains will be able to travel at over 250 km/h on those lines shown on the map.

Ports and ferries

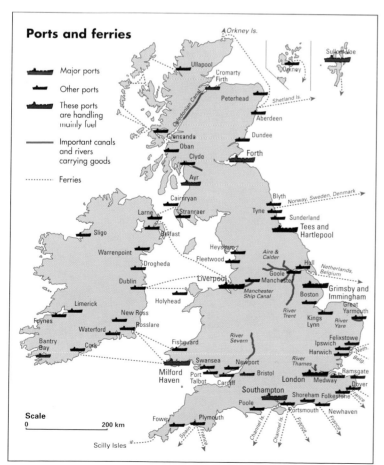

- ⬛ Major ports
- ▪ Other ports
- ⬛ These ports are handling mainly fuel
- ━━ Important canals and rivers carrying goods
- ⋯⋯ Ferries

Scale
0 ___ 200 km

Airports

- ✈ Over half the people are travelling within the UK or Ireland (Domestic airports)
- ✈ Over half the people are travelling to other countries (International airports)

Scale
0 ___ 200 km

Tourism and conservation

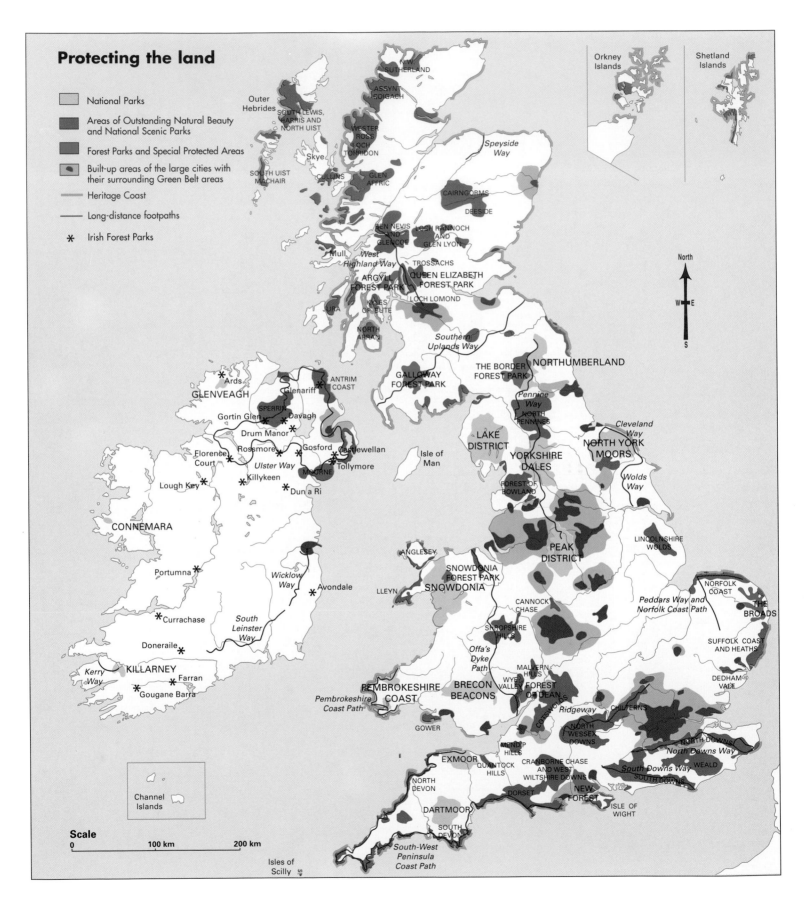

Protecting the land

- National Parks
- Areas of Outstanding Natural Beauty and National Scenic Parks
- Forest Parks and Special Protected Areas
- Built-up areas of the large cities with their surrounding Green Belt areas
- Heritage Coast
- Long-distance footpaths
- * Irish Forest Parks

Orkney Islands

Shetland Islands

Outer Hebrides

N.W. SUTHERLAND

SOUTH LEWIS, HARRIS AND NORTH UIST

ASSYNT COIGACH

WESTER ROSS LOCH TORRIDON

Skye

Speyside Way

SOUTH UIST MACHAIR

CULLINS

GLEN AFFRIC

CAIRNGORMS

DEESIDE

BEN NEVIS AND GLENCOE

LOCH RANNOCH AND GLEN LYON

Mull

West Highland Way

TROSSACHS

North

ARGYLL FOREST PARK

QUEEN ELIZABETH FOREST PARK

W E

JURA

KYLES OF BUTE

LOCH LOMOND

S

NORTH ARRAN

Southern Uplands Way

THE BORDER FOREST PARK

NORTHUMBERLAND

* Ards

GLENVEAGH

Glenariff

ANTRIM COAST

GALLOWAY FOREST PARK

SPERRIN

Gortin Glen *

Davagh

Pennine Way

Cleveland Way

Drum Manor

NORTH PENNINES

Rossmore

Gosford

Castlewellan

LAKE DISTRICT

NORTH YORK MOORS

Florence Court

Ulster Way

MOURNE

Tollymore

Isle of Man

YORKSHIRE DALES

Wolds Way

Lough Key *

* Killykeen

* Dun a Ri

FOREST OF BOWLAND

CONNEMARA

LINCOLNSHIRE WOLDS

PEAK DISTRICT

ANGLESEY

* Portumna

Wicklow Way

* Avondale

SNOWDONIA FOREST PARK

NORFOLK COAST

LLEYN

SNOWDONIA

Peddars Way and Norfolk Coast Path

THE BROADS

* Currachase

South Leinster Way

CANNOCK CHASE

SHROPSHIRE HILLS

SUFFOLK COAST AND HEATHS

Doneraile *

Offa's Dyke Path

MALVERN HILLS

WYE VALLEY

FOREST OF DEAN

DEDHAM VALE

Kerry Way

KILLARNEY

Farran *

PEMBROKESHIRE COAST

BRECON BEACONS

Ridgeway

COTSWOLDS

CHILTERNS

NORTH DOWNS

* Gougane Barra

Pembrokeshire Coast Path

NORTH WESSEX DOWNS

North Downs Way

WEALD

GOWER

MENDIP HILLS

CRANBORNE CHASE AND WEST WILTSHIRE DOWNS

South Downs Way

SOUTH DOWNS

EXMOOR

QUANTOCK HILLS

NEW FOREST

NORTH DEVON

DORSET

ISLE OF WIGHT

Scale
0   100 km   200 km

Channel Islands

DARTMOOR

SOUTH DEVON

Isles of Scilly

South-West Peninsula Coast Path

Holidays in Britain and other countries

millions

Holidays abroad
Holidays in Great Britain

This shows the number of holidays (four nights or more) taken by people who live in Great Britain.

British tourists to other countries 1995

(number of tourists in thousands)

France	**9,700**
Spain	**8,300**
Ireland	**2,800**
USA	**2,500**
Greece	**2,000**
Germany	**1,900**
Italy	**1,600**
Netherlands	**1,300**
Portugal	**1,200**
Belgium	**1,000**
Turkey	**865**
Cyprus	**679**
Austria	**604**
Switzerland	**526**

10 million visitors from UK
7.5 million
5 million
2.5 million
1 million

Tourism

● Main holiday cities and towns

● Major tourist attractions

Scale
0   200 km

Visitors from other countries 1994

(number of visitors in thousands)

USA	**2,979**
France	**2,779**
Germany	**2,517**
Ireland	**1,677**
Netherlands	**1,204**
Belgium–Luxembourg	**1,035**
Italy	**826**
Spain	**697**
Japan	**588**
Canada	**571**
Australia	**562**
Switzerland	**474**
Norway	**336**

Tourist attractions 1995

(number of visitors in millions)

Blackpool Pleasure Beach	**7.3**
British Museum, London	**5.7**
National Gallery, London	**4.5**
Strathclyde Country Park, Glasgow	**4.1**
Brighton Palace Pier	**3.8**
Madame Tussaud's Waxworks, London	**2.7**
Alton Towers, Staffordshire	**2.7**
Tower of London	**2.5**
Trocadero, London	**2.5**
Eastbourne Pier	**2.3**
St Paul's Cathedral, London	**2.2**
Westminster Abbey, London	**2.2**
York Minster	**2.0**
Great Yarmouth Pleasure Beach	**2.0**
Canterbury Cathedral	**1.9**
Chessington World of Adventures	**1.8**
Science Museum, London	**1.6**
Dunstable Downs Country Park	**1.5**
Sandwell Valley Country Park, W. Bromwich	**1.5**

Water

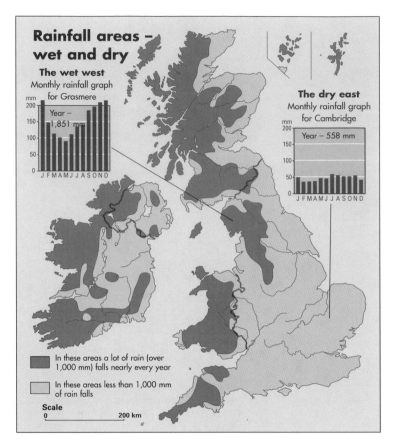

Rainfall areas – wet and dry

The wet west
Monthly rainfall graph for Grasmere

mm
200
150
100
50
0
J F M A M J J A S O N D

Year – 1,851 mm

The dry east
Monthly rainfall graph for Cambridge

mm
200
150
100
50
0
J F M A M J J A S O N D

Year – 558 mm

In these areas a lot of rain (over 1,000 mm) falls nearly every year

In these areas less than 1,000 mm of rain falls

Scale
0   200 km

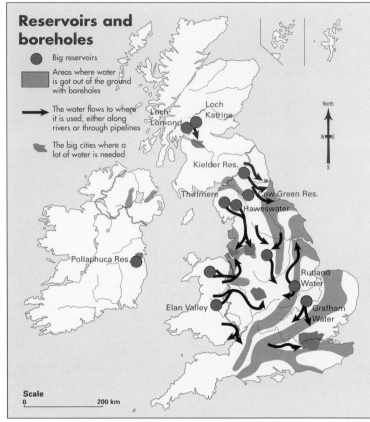

Reservoirs and boreholes

● Big reservoirs

Areas where water is got out of the ground with boreholes

→ The water flows to where it is used, either along rivers or through pipelines

The big cities where a lot of water is needed

North
W — E
S

Loch Lomond
Loch Katrine
Kielder Res.
Thirlmere
Cow Green Res.
Haweswater
Pollaphuca Res.
Rutland Water
Elan Valley
Grafham Water

Scale
0   200 km

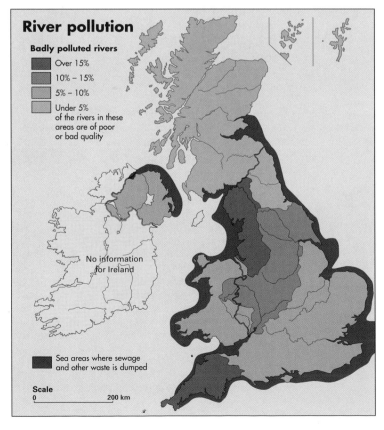

River pollution

Badly polluted rivers

Over 15%

10% – 15%

5% – 10%

Under 5% of the rivers in these areas are of poor or bad quality

No information for Ireland

Sea areas where sewage and other waste is dumped

Scale
0   200 km

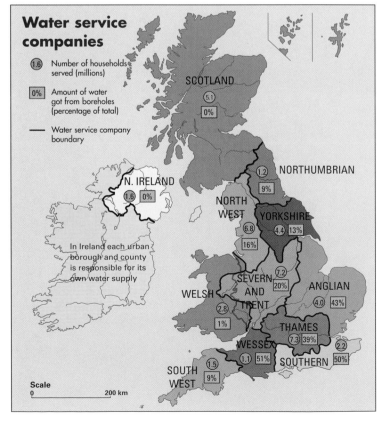

Water service companies

(1.6) Number of households served (millions)

[0%] Amount of water got from boreholes (percentage of total)

— Water service company boundary

SCOTLAND (5.1) [0%]

N. IRELAND (1.6) [0%]

In Ireland each urban borough and county is responsible for its own water supply

NORTHUMBRIAN (1.2) [9%]

NORTH WEST (6.8) [16%]

YORKSHIRE (4.4) [13%]

SEVERN AND TRENT (7.2) [20%]

ANGLIAN (4.0) [43%]

WELSH (2.8) [1%]

THAMES (7.3) [39%]

WESSEX (1.1) [51%]

SOUTHERN (2.2) [50%]

SOUTH WEST (1.5) [9%]

Scale
0   200 km

Water use in the United Kingdom

In 1995 the average UK household used 380 litres of water a day. Up to 135,000 million litres of water are used each day in the UK. Over half the water is used by people in their homes. About a third is used to make electricity. The rest is used in farms and factories. On the right are some of the ways that water is used in the home:

To make one car can use up to 30,000 litres of water. To brew one pint of beer needs 8 pints of water.

Domestic appliances – water usage

	(per wash)
Washing machine	110 litres
Bath	80 litres
Dishwasher	55 litres
Shower	35 litres
Toilet flush	10 litres

The water cycle

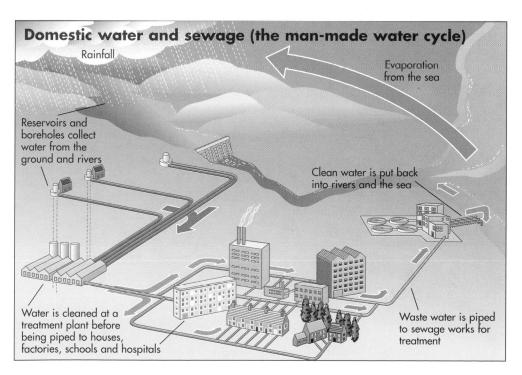

Condensation

Moist air mass moves to land

Precipitation

Transpiration from vegetation

Evaporation from ponds and lakes

Evaporation from soil

Evaporation from rivers

Evaporation from oceans

Ground water moves to rivers, lakes and oceans

Run off

Ocean

Domestic water and sewage (the man-made water cycle)

Rainfall

Evaporation from the sea

Reservoirs and boreholes collect water from the ground and rivers

Clean water is put back into rivers and the sea

Water is cleaned at a treatment plant before being piped to houses, factories, schools and hospitals

Waste water is piped to sewage works for treatment

Acid rain in Britain

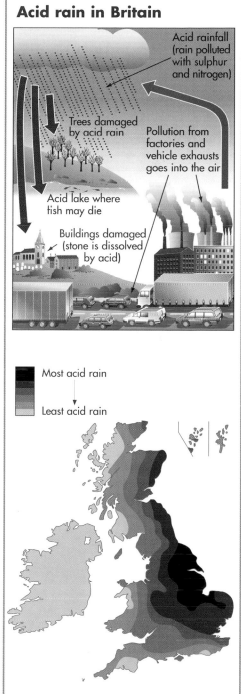

Acid rainfall (rain polluted with sulphur and nitrogen)

Trees damaged by acid rain

Pollution from factories and vehicle exhausts goes into the air

Acid lake where fish may die

Buildings damaged (stone is dissolved by acid)

Most acid rain

Least acid rain

Names

The map on the left shows the **British Isles**, which is made up of the two large islands of **Great Britain** and **Ireland** and many smaller islands. There are two countries, the **United Kingdom** and **Ireland**. The full name of the United Kingdom is The United Kingdom of Great Britain and Northern Ireland. It has four parts: **England**, **Wales**, **Scotland** and **Northern Ireland**. It is known for short as the United Kingdom, UK or Britain. The whole country is often wrongly called England. The republic of Ireland is sometimes shown as Eire (on its stamps), which is the name of Ireland in the Irish language.

These are the names for some of the different areas in the British Isles

Counties and regions

The map shows the Standard Regions of the United Kingdom. The boundaries follow those of the counties shown on page 23. Large bodies like the Health Service, Water or Electricity divide the country up into their own regions. Ireland is divided into four historic provinces.

Counties and unitary authorities

England and Wales are divided into counties, unitary authorities and boroughs. The counties are divided into districts, and the districts into parishes and wards. Scotland is divided into regions and unitary authorities, and Northern Ireland into districts.

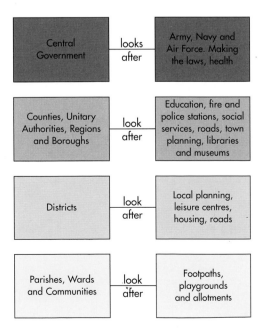

Central Government	looks after	Army, Navy and Air Force. Making the laws, health
Counties, Unitary Authorities, Regions and Boroughs	look after	Education, fire and police stations, social services, roads, town planning, libraries and museums
Districts	look after	Local planning, leisure centres, housing, roads
Parishes, Wards and Communities	look after	Footpaths, playgrounds and allotments

Area data

	Area in square kilometres
England	130,439
Wales	20,768
Scotland	77,167
Northern Ireland	13,483
United Kingdom	**241,857**
Isle of Man	**572**
Channel Islands	**195**
Ireland	**68,896**

The Channel Islands and the Isle of Man are dependencies of the Crown and have their own parliaments. They are not part of the United Kingdom.

The six counties are shown in Northern Ireland. It is divided for local government into 26 districts.

The map shows the 6 counties in Northern Ireland, the 32 unitary authorities in Scotland, the 22 unitary authorities in Wales, and the 87 unitary authorities in England as of 1 April 1998. Authorities which are too small to name on the map are numbered and listed separately.

SCOTLAND
1. ABERDEEN CITY
2. DUNDEE CITY
3. WEST DUNBARTONSHIRE
4. EAST DUNBARTONSHIRE
5. CITY OF GLASGOW
6. INVERCLYDE
7. RENFREWSHIRE
8. EAST RENFREWSHIRE
9. NORTH LANARKSHIRE
10. FALKIRK
11. CLACKMANNANSHIRE
12. WEST LOTHIAN
13. CITY OF EDINBURGH
14. MIDLOTHIAN

WALES
15. SWANSEA
16. NEATH PORT TALBOT
17. BRIDGEND
18. RHONDDA CYNON TAFF
19. MERTHYR TYDFIL
20. CAERPHILLY
21. BLAENAU GWENT
22. TORFAEN
23. CARDIFF
24. NEWPORT

ENGLAND
25. HARTLEPOOL
26. DARLINGTON
27. STOCKTON-ON-TEES
28. MIDDLESBROUGH
29. REDCAR AND CLEVELAND
30. BLACKPOOL
31. BLACKBURN WITH DARWEN
32. HALTON
33. WARRINGTON
34. KINGSTON UPON HULL
35. NORTH EAST LINCOLNSHIRE
36. STOKE-ON-TRENT
37. TELFORD AND WREKIN
38. DERBY CITY
39. CITY OF NOTTINGHAM
40. LEICESTER CITY
41. RUTLAND
42. PETERBOROUGH
43. MILTON KEYNES
44. LUTON
45. NORTH SOMERSET
46. CITY OF BRISTOL
47. BATH AND N. E. SOMERSET
48. SWINDON
49. READING
50. WOKINGHAM
51. WINDSOR AND MAIDENHEAD
52. SLOUGH
53. BRACKNELL FOREST
54. THURROCK
55. SOUTHEND-ON-SEA
56. MEDWAY TOWNS
57. PLYMOUTH
58. TORBAY
59. POOLE
60. BOURNEMOUTH
61. SOUTHAMPTON
62. PORTSMOUTH
63. BRIGHTON AND HOVE

Scale
0   100 km   200 km

• Capital cities

FRANCE

CHANNEL ISLANDS
St. Peter Port
Guernsey   FRANCE
Jersey
St. Helier

23

England and Wales

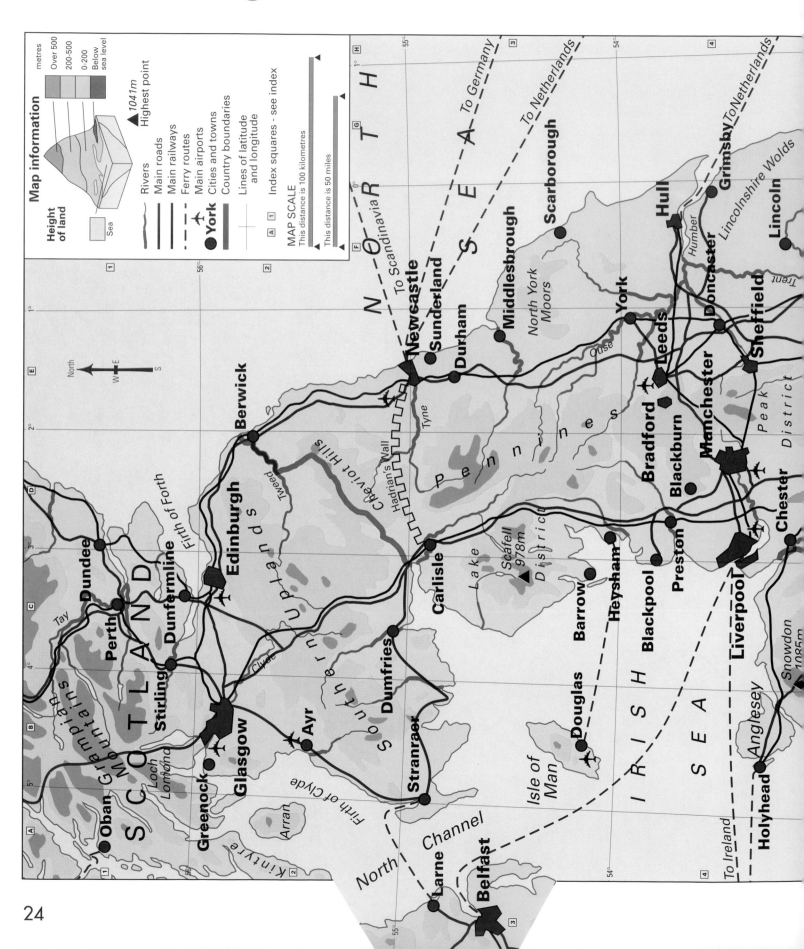

Map information

Height of land

metres	
Over 500	
200–500	
0–200	
Below sea level	

▲ 1041m Highest point

Sea

Rivers
Main roads
Main railways
Ferry routes
Main airports
● **York** Cities and towns
Country boundaries
Lines of latitude and longitude

A 1 Index squares – see index

MAP SCALE
This distance is 100 kilometres
This distance is 50 miles

North
W — E
S

NORTH SEA

To Scandinavia
To Germany
To Netherlands
To Netherlands

Newcastle
Sunderland
Durham
Middlesbrough
Scarborough
North York Moors
York
Ouse
Hull
Humber
Doncaster
Grimsby
Lincolnshire Wolds
Lincoln
Trent
Sheffield
Leeds
Bradford
Blackburn
Manchester
Peak District
Chester
Preston
Blackpool
Heysham
Barrow
Liverpool
Snowdon 1085m
Anglesey
Holyhead
To Ireland

Berwick
Tweed
Cheviot Hills
Hadrian's Wall
Tyne
Pennines
Carlisle
Lake District
Scafell 978m

Edinburgh
Firth of Forth
Dunfermline
Southern Uplands
Dumfries
Stranraer
Clyde

SCOTLAND
Oban
Grampian Mountains
Tay
Dundee
Perth
Stirling
Loch Lomond
Greenock
Glasgow
Ayr
Arran
Firth of Clyde
Kintyre

IRISH SEA

Isle of Man
Douglas

North Channel
Larne
Belfast

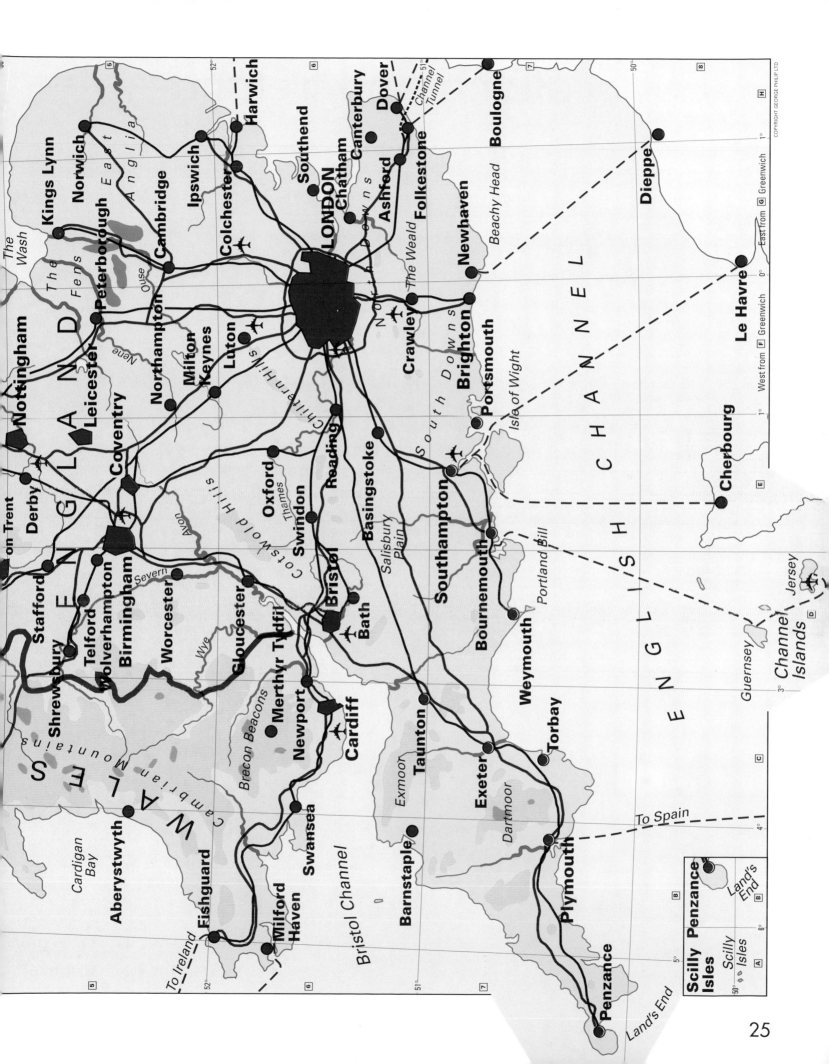

25

Scotland and Ireland

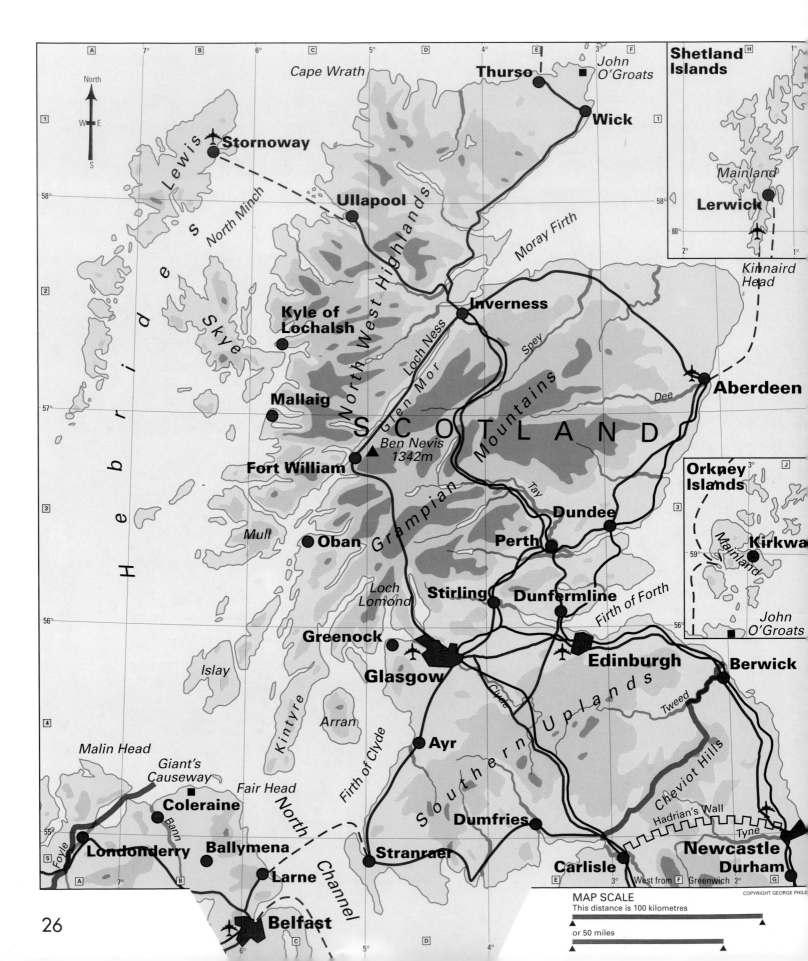

MAP SCALE
This distance is 100 kilometres

or 50 miles

COPYRIGHT GEORGE PHILIP

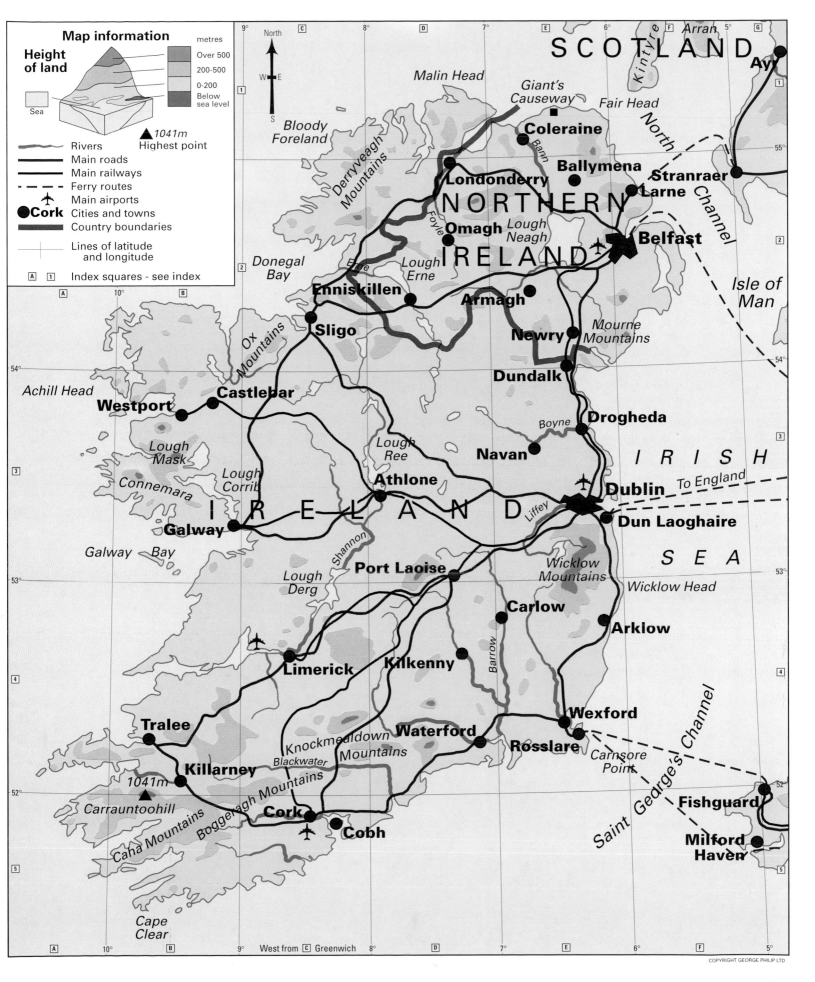

Map information

Height of land

	metres
	Over 500
	200-500
	0-200
	Below sea level

Sea

▲1041m Highest point

Rivers
Main roads
Main railways
Ferry routes
✈ Main airports
● **Cork** Cities and towns
Country boundaries
Lines of latitude and longitude

Ⓐ ① Index squares - see index

SCOTLAND

Ayr

Malin Head

Bloody Foreland

Giant's Causeway

Fair Head

Coleraine

Bann

Ballymena

Londonderry

Foyle

NORTHERN

Omagh

Lough Neagh

IRELAND

Belfast

Stranraer

Larne

North Channel

Isle of Man

Derryveagh Mountains

Erne

Donegal Bay

Lough Erne

Enniskillen

Armagh

Sligo

Newry

Mourne Mountains

Ox Mountains

Dundalk

Achill Head

Westport

Castlebar

Boyne

Drogheda

Lough Mask

Lough Ree

Navan

IRISH

Lough Corrib

Connemara

Athlone

Dublin

To England

Galway

I R E L A N D

Liffey

Dun Laoghaire

Galway Bay

SEA

Shannon

Lough Derg

Port Laoise

Wicklow Mountains

Wicklow Head

Carlow

Arklow

Barrow

Limerick

Kilkenny

Tralee

Waterford

Wexford

Knockmealdown Mountains

Rosslare

Carnsore Point

Saint George's Channel

Blackwater

Killarney

1041m ▲

Carrauntoohill

Caha Mountains

Boggeragh Mountains

Cork

Cobh

Fishguard

Milford Haven

Cape Clear

West from Ⓒ Greenwich

The Earth as a planet

Relative sizes of the planets

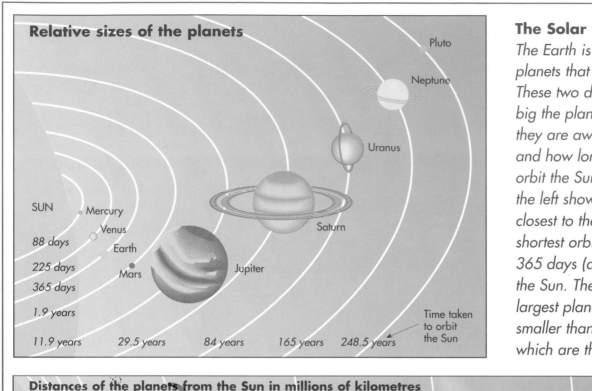

SUN

Mercury
Venus
Earth
Mars
Jupiter
Saturn
Uranus
Neptune
Pluto

88 days
225 days
365 days
1.9 years
11.9 years   29.5 years   84 years   165 years   248.5 years

Time taken to orbit the Sun

The Solar System
The Earth is one of the nine planets that orbit the Sun. These two diagrams show how big the planets are, how far they are away from the Sun and how long they take to orbit the Sun. The diagram on the left shows how the planets closest to the Sun have the shortest orbits. The Earth takes 365 days (a year) to go round the Sun. The Earth is the fifth largest planet. It is much smaller than Jupiter and Saturn which are the largest planets.

Distances of the planets from the Sun in millions of kilometres

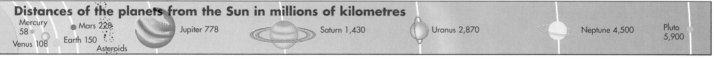

Mercury 58
Venus 108
Earth 150
Mars 228
Asteroids
Jupiter 778
Saturn 1,430
Uranus 2,870
Neptune 4,500
Pluto 5,900

Planet Earth

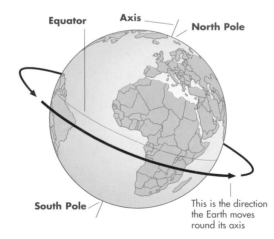

Equator   Axis   North Pole
South Pole
This is the direction the Earth moves round its axis

The Earth spins as if it is on a rod – its axis. The axis would come out of the Earth at two points. The northern point is called the North Pole and the southern point is called the South Pole. The distance between the Poles through the centre of the Earth is 12,700 km.

It takes a day (24 hours) for the Earth to rotate on its axis. It is light (day) when it faces the Sun and dark (night) when it faces away. See the diagram below. The Equator is a line round the Earth which is halfway between the Poles. It is 40,000 km long.

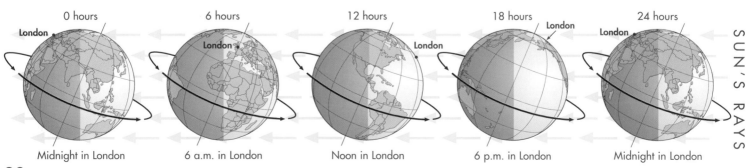

0 hours   6 hours   12 hours   18 hours   24 hours
London   London   London   London   London
Midnight in London   6 a.m. in London   Noon in London   6 p.m. in London   Midnight in London

SUN'S RAYS

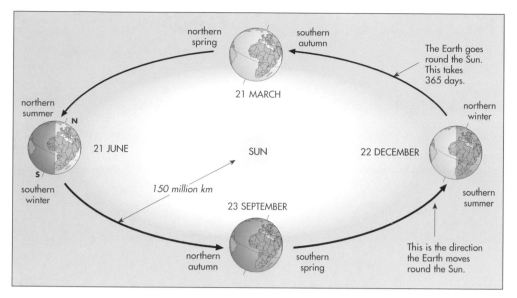

The year and seasons

The Earth is always tilted at $66\frac{1}{2}°$. It moves around the Sun. This movement gives us the seasons of the year. In June the northern hemisphere tilts towards the Sun so it is summer. Six months later, in December, the Earth has rotated halfway round the Sun. It is then summer in the southern hemisphere.

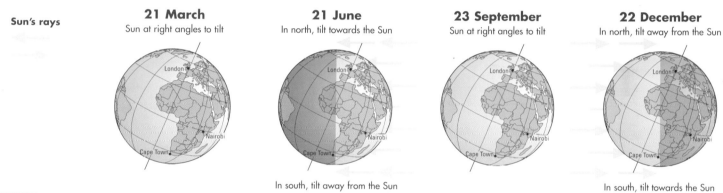

| **Sun's rays** | **21 March** Sun at right angles to tilt | **21 June** In north, tilt towards the Sun | **23 September** Sun at right angles to tilt | **22 December** In north, tilt away from the Sun |

In south, tilt away from the Sun

In south, tilt towards the Sun

Season	Northern Spring Southern Autumn			Northern Summer Southern Winter			Northern Autumn Southern Spring			Northern Winter Southern Summer		
City	London	Nairobi	Cape Town	London	Nairobi	Cape Town	London	Nairobi	Cape Town	London	Nairobi	Cape Town
Latitude	51°N	1°S	34°S	51°N	1°S	34°S	51°N	1°S	34°S	51°N	1°S	34°S
Day length	12 hrs	12 hrs	12 hrs	16 hrs	12 hrs	10 hrs	12 hrs	12 hrs	12 hrs	8 hrs	12 hrs	14 hrs
Night length	12 hrs	12 hrs	12 hrs	8 hrs	12 hrs	14 hrs	12 hrs	12 hrs	12 hrs	16 hrs	12 hrs	10 hrs
Temperature	7°C	21°C	21°C	16°C	18°C	13°C	15°C	19°C	14°C	5°C	19°C	20°C

For example, at London in spring and autumn there are 12 hours of day and 12 hours of night. In winter this becomes 8 hours and in the summer 16 hours.

The Moon

The Moon is about a quarter the size of the Earth. It orbits the Earth in just over 27 days (almost a month). The Moon is round but we on Earth see only the parts lit by the Sun. This makes it look as if the Moon is a different shape at different times of the month. These are known as the phases of the Moon and they are shown in this diagram.

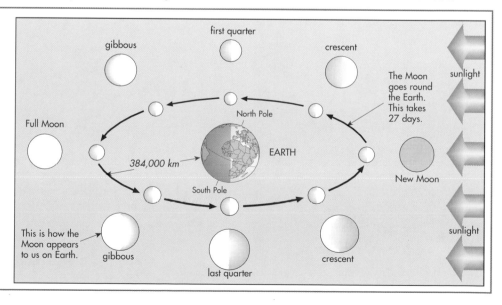

Mountains and rivers

The surface of the Earth is continually being shaped by movements of the Earth's crust. Volcanoes are formed and earthquakes are caused in this way. Rivers also shape the landscape as they flow on their way to the sea.

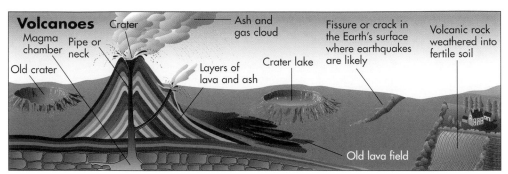

Volcanoes
Crater
Magma chamber
Pipe or neck
Old crater
Ash and gas cloud
Layers of lava and ash
Crater lake
Fissure or crack in the Earth's surface where earthquakes are likely
Volcanic rock weathered into fertile soil
Old lava field

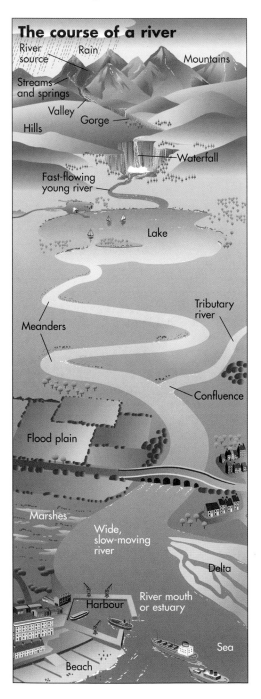

The course of a river
River source
Rain
Mountains
Streams and springs
Valley
Gorge
Hills
Waterfall
Fast-flowing young river
Lake
Tributary river
Meanders
Confluence
Flood plain
Marshes
Wide, slow-moving river
Delta
Harbour
River mouth or estuary
Beach
Sea

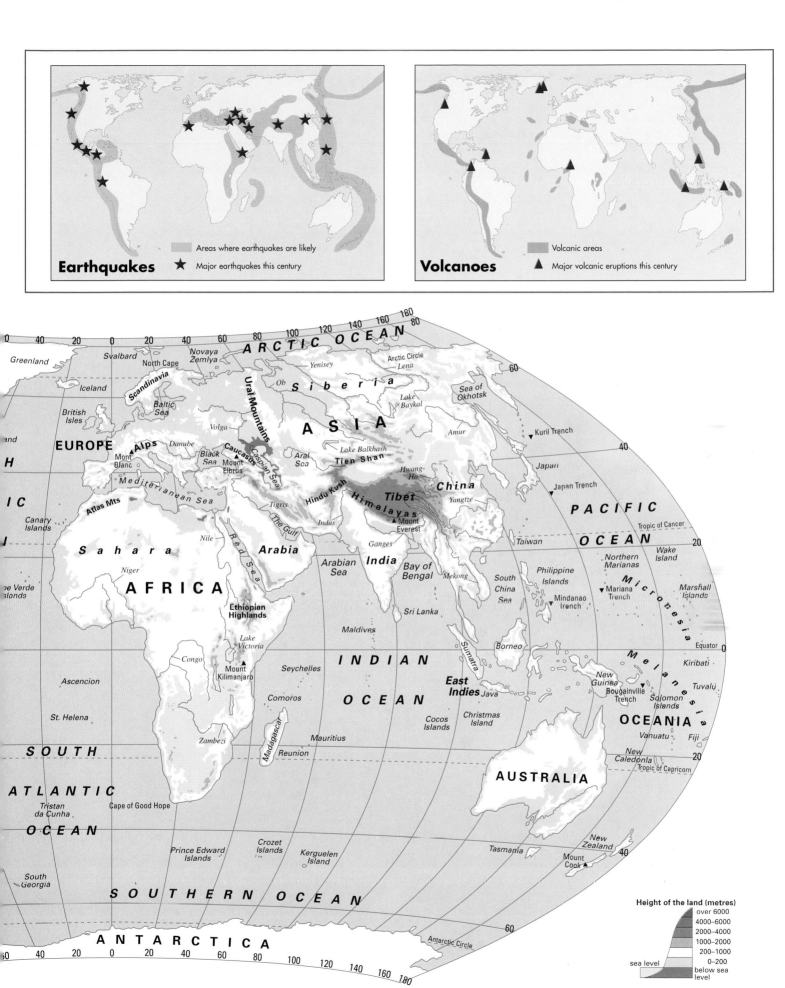

Earthquakes

Areas where earthquakes are likely

★ Major earthquakes this century

Volcanoes

Volcanic areas

▲ Major volcanic eruptions this century

Greenland
Svalbard
Novaya Zemlya
North Cape
ARCTIC OCEAN
Arctic Circle
Yenisey
Lena
Iceland
Scandinavia
Ob
Siberia
60
British Isles
Baltic Sea
Ural Mountains
Lake Baykal
Sea of Okhotsk
EUROPE
Alps
Danube
Volga
Caucasus
ASIA
Amur
Kuril Trench
40
Mont Blanc
Black Sea
Mount Elbrus
Caspian Sea
Aral Sea
Lake Balkhash
Tien Shan
Japan
Mediterranean Sea
Tigris
Hindu Kush
Hwang-Ho
Japan Trench
Atlas Mts
Nile
The Gulf
Tibet
China
PACIFIC
Canary Islands
Sahara
Indus
Himalayas
Yangtze
Tropic of Cancer
OCEAN
20
Arabia
Mount Everest
Taiwan
Niger
Ganges
India
Wake Island
Cape Verde Islands
AFRICA
Arabian Sea
Bay of Bengal
Mekong
Philippine Islands
Northern Marianas
Micronesia
Marshall Islands
Mindanao Trench
Mariana Trench
South China Sea
Ethiopian Highlands
Sri Lanka
Equator
0
Ascencion
Congo
Lake Victoria
Maldives
INDIAN
Borneo
Melanesia
Kiribati
New Guinea
St. Helena
Mount Kilimanjaro
Seychelles
OCEAN
East Indies
Java
Bougainville Trench
Solomon Islands
Tuvalu
Comoros
Sumatra
OCEANIA
Zambezi
Madagascar
Mauritius
Cocos Islands
Christmas Island
Vanuatu
Fiji
SOUTH
Reunion
New Caledonia
20
ATLANTIC
Tristan da Cunha
Cape of Good Hope
Tropic of Capricorn
OCEAN
AUSTRALIA
South Georgia
Prince Edward Islands
Crozet Islands
Kerguelen Island
Tasmania
New Zealand
40
Mount Cook
SOUTHERN OCEAN
60
Antarctic Circle
ANTARCTICA

Height of the land (metres)

over 6000
4000–6000
2000–4000
1000–2000
200–1000
0–200
sea level
below sea level

Climates of the World

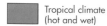
Tropical climate (hot and wet)

Heavy rainfall and high temperatures all the year with little difference between the hot and cold months.

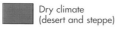
Dry climate (desert and steppe)

Many months, often years, without rain. High temperatures in the summer but cooler in winter.

Mild climate (warm and wet)

Rain every month. Warm summers and cool winters.

Continental climate (cold and wet)

Mild summers and very cold winters.

Polar climate (very cold and dry)

Very cold at all times, especially in the winter months. Very little rainfall.

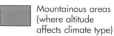
Mountainous areas (where altitude affects climate type)

Lower temperatures because the land is high. Heavy rain and snow.

Key to the climate graphs

Total annual rainfall

Average monthly rainfall

Months of the year from January to December

Average monthly temperature in degrees C. When the temperature is below freezing the lines extend below the bottom of the graph.

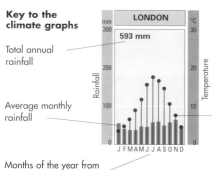

LONDON — 593 mm

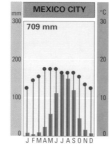

MEXICO CITY — 709 mm

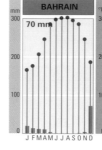

BAHRAIN — 70 mm

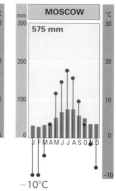

MOSCOW — 575 mm — −10°C

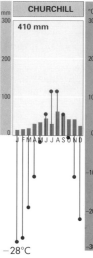

CHURCHILL — 410 mm — −28°C

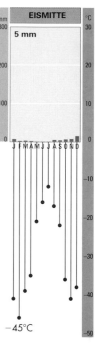

EISMITTE — 5 mm — −45°C

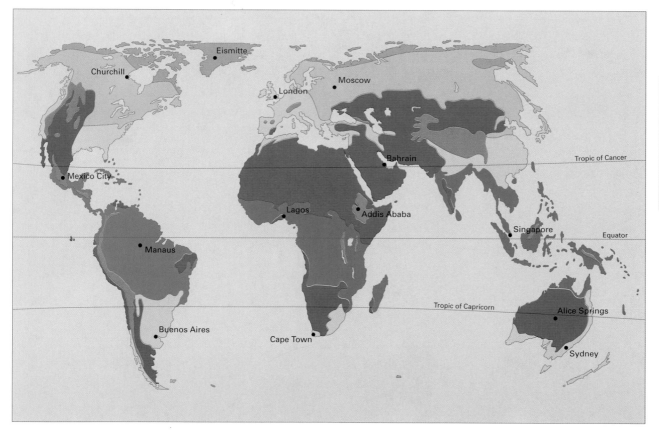

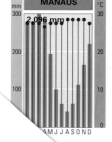

MANAUS — 2,096 mm

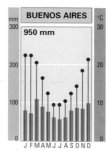

BUENOS AIRES — 950 mm

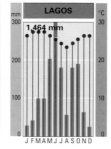

LAGOS — 1,464 mm

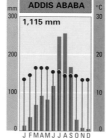

ADDIS ABABA — 1,115 mm

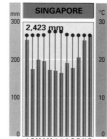

SINGAPORE — 2,423 mm

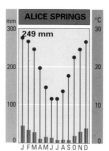

ALICE SPRINGS — 249 mm

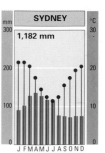

SYDNEY — 1,182 mm

Annual rainfall

Human, plant and animal life cannot live without water. The map on the right shows how much rain falls in different parts of the world. You can see that there is a lot of rain in some places near the Equator. In other places, like the desert areas of the world, there is very little rain. Few plants or animals can survive there. There is also very little rain in the cold lands of the north.

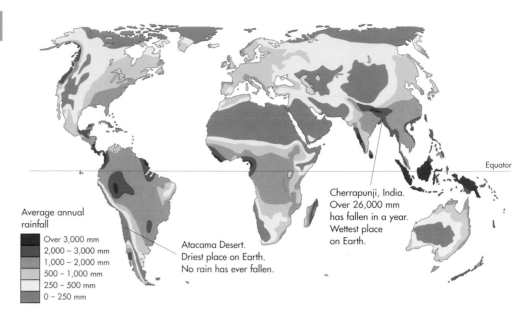

Average annual rainfall

- Over 3,000 mm
- 2,000 – 3,000 mm
- 1,000 – 2,000 mm
- 500 – 1,000 mm
- 250 – 500 mm
- 0 – 250 mm

Equator

Cherrapunji, India. Over 26,000 mm has fallen in a year. Wettest place on Earth.

Atacama Desert. Driest place on Earth. No rain has ever fallen.

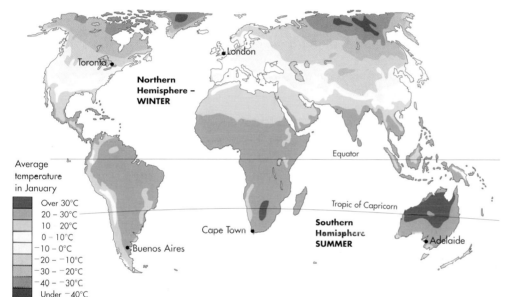

Average temperature in January

- Over 30°C
- 20 – 30°C
- 10 – 20°C
- 0 – 10°C
- −10 – 0°C
- −20 – −10°C
- −30 – −20°C
- −40 – −30°C
- Under −40°C

Toronto

London

Northern Hemisphere – WINTER

Equator

Tropic of Capricorn

Cape Town

Buenos Aires

Southern Hemisphere SUMMER

Adelaide

January temperature

In December, it is winter in the northern hemisphere. It is hot in the southern continents and cold in the northern continents. The North Pole is tilted away from the sun. It is overhead in the regions around the Tropic of Capricorn. This means that there are about 14 hours of daylight in Buenos Aires, Cape Town and Adelaide, and only about 8 hours in London and Toronto.

June temperature

In June, it is summer in the northern hemisphere and winter in the southern hemisphere. It is warmer in the northern lands and colder in the south. The North Pole is tilted towards the sun. This means that in London and Toronto there are about 16 hours of daylight, but in Buenos Aires, Cape Town and Adelaide there are just under 10 hours.

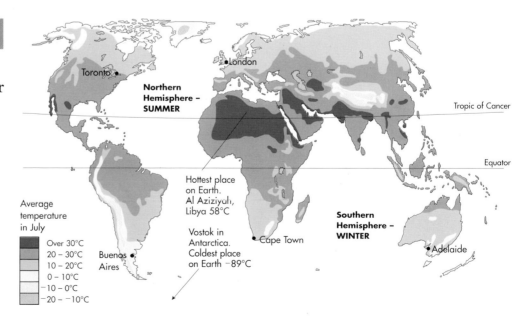

Average temperature in July

- Over 30°C
- 20 – 30°C
- 10 – 20°C
- 0 – 10°C
- −10 – 0°C
- −20 – −10°C

Toronto

London

Northern Hemisphere – SUMMER

Tropic of Cancer

Equator

Hottest place on Earth. Al Aziziyah, Libya 58°C

Vostok in Antarctica. Coldest place on Earth −89°C

Buenos Aires

Cape Town

Southern Hemisphere – WINTER

Adelaide

– Forests, grasslands and wastes –

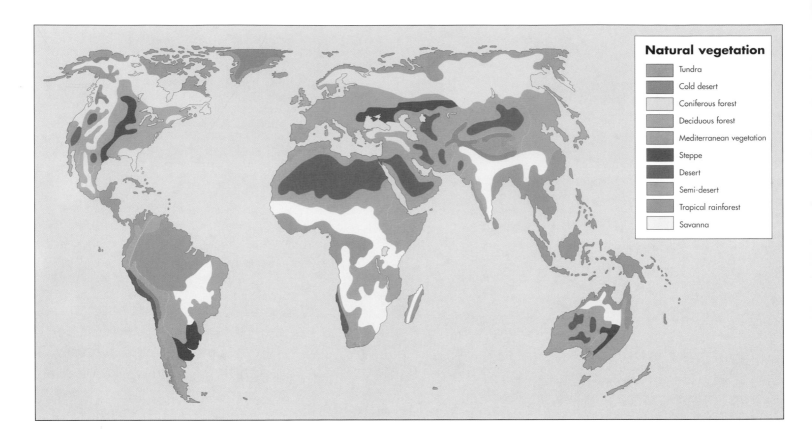

Natural vegetation

- Tundra
- Cold desert
- Coniferous forest
- Deciduous forest
- Mediterranean vegetation
- Steppe
- Desert
- Semi-desert
- Tropical rainforest
- Savanna

The map above shows types of vegetation around the world. The diagram below shows the types of plants which grow on mountains.

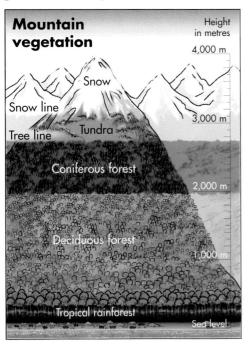

Mountain vegetation

Height in metres

4,000 m

Snow

Snow line

Tree line

Tundra

3,000 m

Coniferous forest

2,000 m

Deciduous forest

1,000 m

Tropical rainforest

Sea level

Tundra

Long, dry, cold winters. Grasses, moss, bog and dwarf trees.

Coniferous forest

Harsh winters, mild summers. Trees have leaves all year.

Mediterranean

Hot, dry summers. Mild wet winters. Plants adapt to the heat.

Desert

Rain is rare. Plants only grow at oases with underground water.

Tropical rainforest (jungle)

Very hot and wet all the year. Tall trees and lush vegetation.

Cold desert

Very cold with little rain or snow. No plants can grow.

Deciduous forest

Rain all year, cool winters. Trees shed leaves in winter.

Steppe

Some rain with a dry season. Grasslands with some trees.

Semi-desert

Poor rains, sparse vegetation. Grass with a few small trees.

Savanna

Mainly dry, but lush grass grows when the rains come.

Tundra

Pingo (mound)

Thin, stony soil with permafrost below

Mosses, lichens and herbs

Cold desert

No plants can grow

Coniferous forest

Evergreen conifers (spruces and firs)

Young tree saplings and small shrubs

Carpet of pine needles

Ferns and brambles on edge of forest

Yearly cycle of a deciduous forest

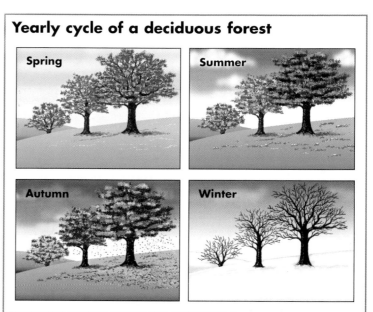

Spring

Summer

Autumn

Winter

Mediterranean

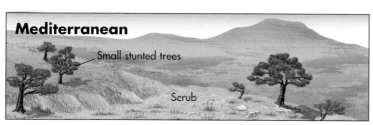

Small stunted trees

Scrub

Steppe

There are many plants in the steppe grasslands.

People planting crops damages the natural habitat.

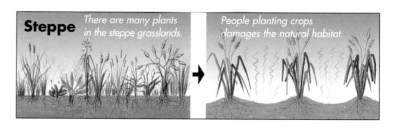

Tropical rainforest

Scattered trees with umbrella-shaped tops grow the highest.

Main layer of tall trees growing close together.

Creepers grow up the trees to reach the sunlight.

Ferns, mosses and small plants grow closest to the ground.

Desert

Palm trees

Cactus

Sand blown into dunes by the wind

Oasis

Semi-desert

Joshua trees

Grass and bush

Savanna

Dry season

Wet season

- Agriculture, forests and fishing -

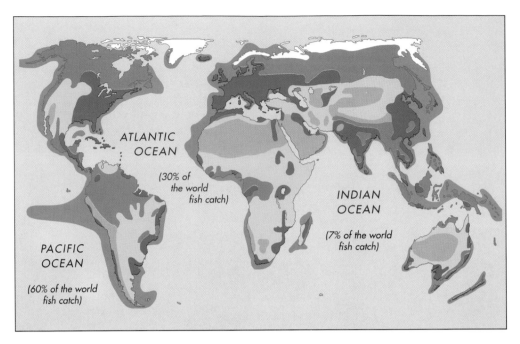

ATLANTIC OCEAN

(30% of the world fish catch)

PACIFIC OCEAN

(60% of the world fish catch)

INDIAN OCEAN

(7% of the world fish catch)

How the land is used

Forest areas with timber. Some hunting and fishing. Agriculture in the tropics.

Deserts and wastelands. Some small areas of agriculture in oases or places that have been irrigated.

Animal farming on large farms (ranches)

Farming of crops and animals on large and small farms

Main fishing areas

The importance of agriculture

Over half the people work in agriculture

Between a quarter and half the people work in agriculture

Between one in ten and a quarter of the people work in agriculture

Less than one in ten of the people work in agriculture

● Countries which depend on agriculture for over half their income

A hundred years ago about 80% of the world's population worked in agriculture. Today it is only about 40% but agriculture is still very important in some countries.

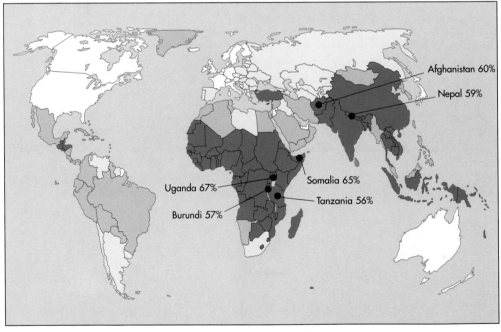

Afghanistan 60%

Nepal 59%

Somalia 65%

Uganda 67%

Tanzania 56%

Burundi 57%

Methods of fishing

There are two types of sea fishing:

1. **Deep-sea fishing** using large trawlers which often stay at sea for many weeks.

2. **Inshore fishing** using small boats, traps and nets up to 70 km from the coast.

Inshore fishing

Lobster pots

Fish trap

Sonar is used to find fish

Deep-sea fishing (drifter)

Fishing vessels

(trawler)

Seine net to catch herring, tuna and mackerel

Trawl net to catch fish near the sea bed (sole, cod and haddock)

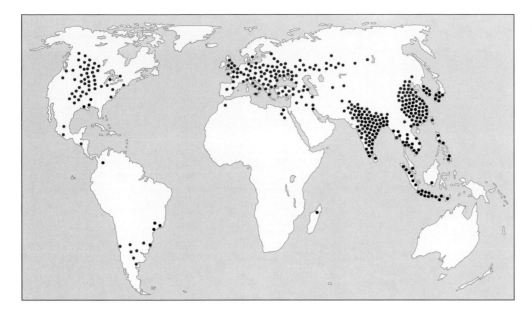

Wheat and rice

- One dot stands for 2 million tonnes of wheat produced

- One dot stands for 2 million tonnes of rice produced

Wheat is the main cereal crop grown in cooler regions. Rice is the main food for over half the people in the world. It is grown in water in paddy fields in tropical areas. Over a third of the world's rice is grown in China.

Cattle and sheep

- One dot stands for 10 million cattle

- One dot stands for 10 million sheep

Meat, milk and leather come from cattle. The map shows that they are kept in most parts of the world except where it is hot or very cold. Sheep are kept in cooler regions and they can live on poorer grassland than cows. Sheep are reared for meat and wool.

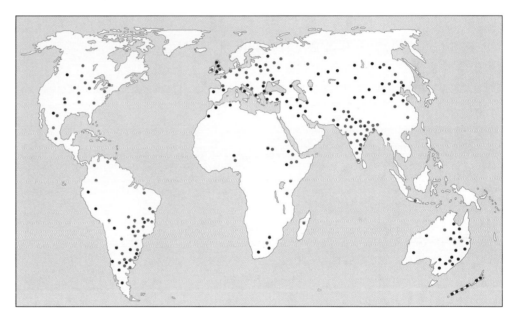

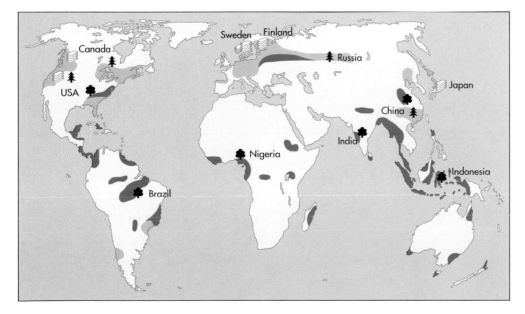

Timber

Main areas where trees are grown for hardwoods (non-coniferous)

Main areas where trees are grown for softwoods (coniferous)

Countries producing over 5% of
the world's hardwood
the world's softwood
the world's wood pulp

Trees are cut down to make timber. Softwood trees such as pines and firs often have cones so they are called coniferous. Some trees are chopped up into wood pulp which is used to make paper.

Minerals and energy

Important metals

- ■ Iron ore
- ▲ Bauxite
- ● Copper

Iron is the most important metal in manufacturing. It is mixed with other metals to make steel which is used for ships, cars and machinery. Bauxite ore is used to make aluminium. Aluminium is light and strong. It is used to make aeroplanes. Copper is used for electric wires, and also to make brass and bronze.

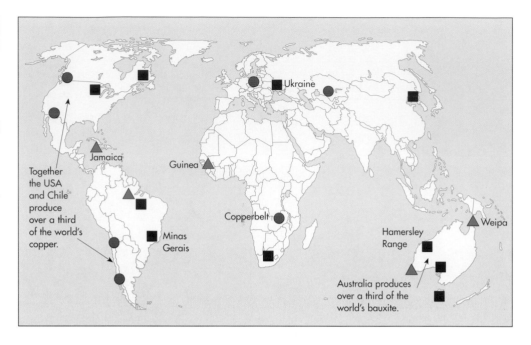

Together the USA and Chile produce over a third of the world's copper.

Australia produces over a third of the world's bauxite.

Ukraine
Jamaica
Guinea
Copperbelt
Hamersley Range
Weipa
Minas Gerais

Precious metals and minerals

- Gold
- ★ Silver
- ◆ Diamonds

Some minerals like gold, silver and diamonds are used to make jewellery. They are also important in industry. Diamonds are the hardest mineral and so they are used on tools that cut or grind. Silver is used in photography to coat film, and to make electrical goods. Gold is used in the electronics industry.

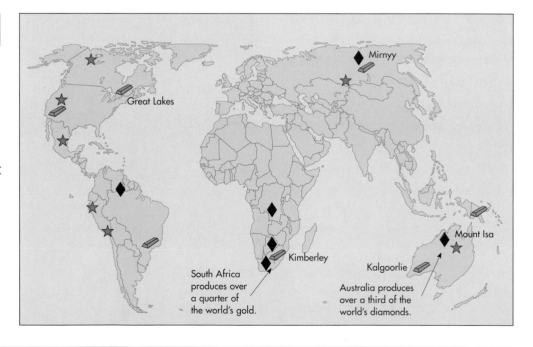

Mirnyy
Great Lakes
Kimberley
South Africa produces over a quarter of the world's gold.
Mount Isa
Kalgoorlie
Australia produces over a third of the world's diamonds.

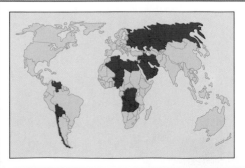

There are over 70 different types of metals and minerals in the world. The maps above show the main countries where some of the most important ones are mined. After mining, metals and fuels are often exported to other countries where they are manufactured into goods. The map on the left shows which countries depend most on mining for their exports and wealth. These countries are coloured red.

Oil and gas

 Oilfields

 Natural gasfields

Main routes for transporting oil and gas by tanker

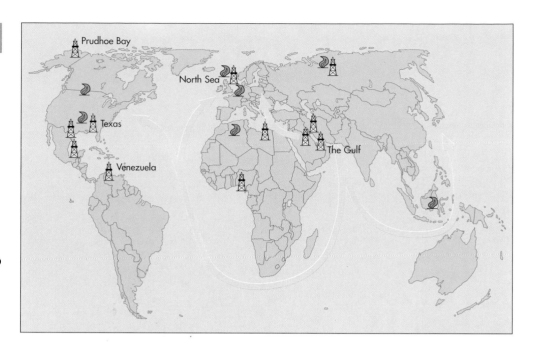

Crude oil is drilled from deep in the Earth's crust. The oil is then refined so that it can be used in different industries. Oil is used to make petrol and is also very important in the chemical industry. Natural gas is often found in the same places as oil.

Coal

▲ Lignite (soft brown coal)

▲ Hard coal (bituminous)

Main routes for transporting coal

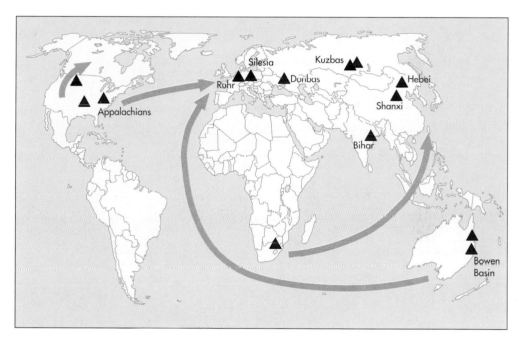

Coal is a fuel that comes from forests and swamps that rotted millions of years ago and have been crushed by layers of rock. The coal is cut out of the rock from deep mines and also from open-cast mines where the coal is nearer the surface. The oldest type of coal is hard. The coal formed more recently is softer.

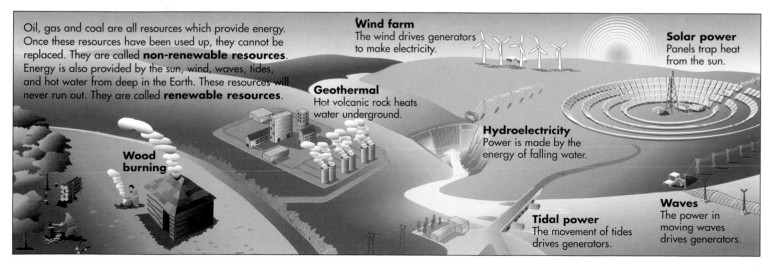

Oil, gas and coal are all resources which provide energy. Once these resources have been used up, they cannot be replaced. They are called **non-renewable resources**. Energy is also provided by the sun, wind, waves, tides, and hot water from deep in the Earth. These resources will never run out. They are called **renewable resources**.

Wind farm
The wind drives generators to make electricity.

Solar power
Panels trap heat from the sun.

Geothermal
Hot volcanic rock heats water underground.

Hydroelectricity
Power is made by the energy of falling water.

Wood burning

Tidal power
The movement of tides drives generators.

Waves
The power in moving waves drives generators.

– Peoples and cities of the World –

Where people live

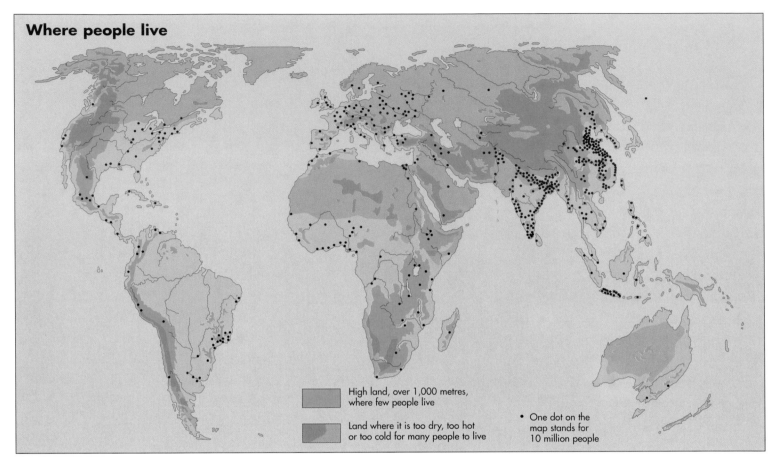

High land, over 1,000 metres, where few people live

Land where it is too dry, too hot or too cold for many people to live

• One dot on the map stands for 10 million people

The growth of the population of the world 1000–2000 AD

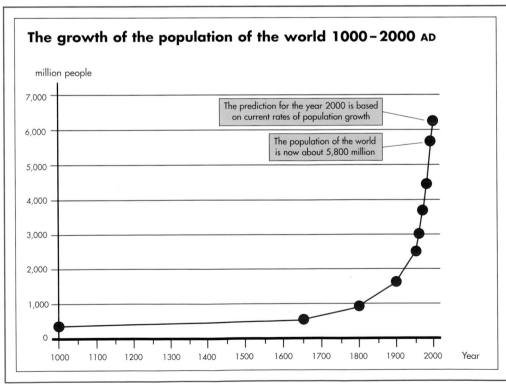

million people

The prediction for the year 2000 is based on current rates of population growth

The population of the world is now about 5,800 million

Year

The population of the continents (1996)

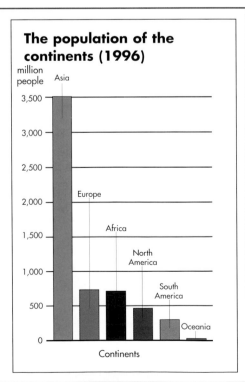

million people

Asia

Europe

Africa

North America

South America

Oceania

Continents

The world's largest cities (1996)

(population in millions)

Tokyo	27
Sao Paulo	16
New York	16
Mexico City	16
Bombay (Mumbai)	15
Shanghai	15
Los Angeles	12
Beijing	12
Calcutta	12
Seoul	12
Jakarta	12
Buenos Aires	11
Tianjin	11
Osaka	11
Lagos	10
Rio de Janeiro	10
Delhi	10
Karachi	10
Cairo	10
Paris	9
Manila	9
Moscow	9
Chicago	8
Dhaka	8
Istanbul	7
London	7

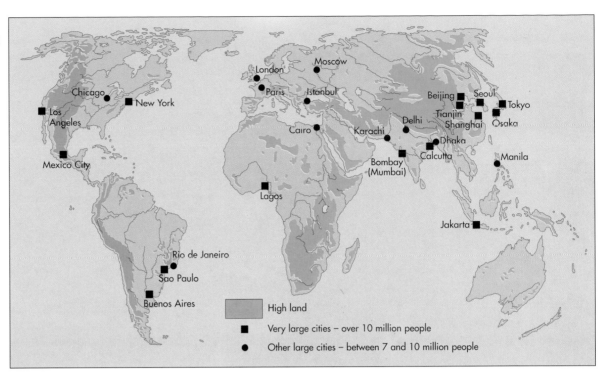

High land

■ Very large cities – over 10 million people

● Other large cities – between 7 and 10 million people

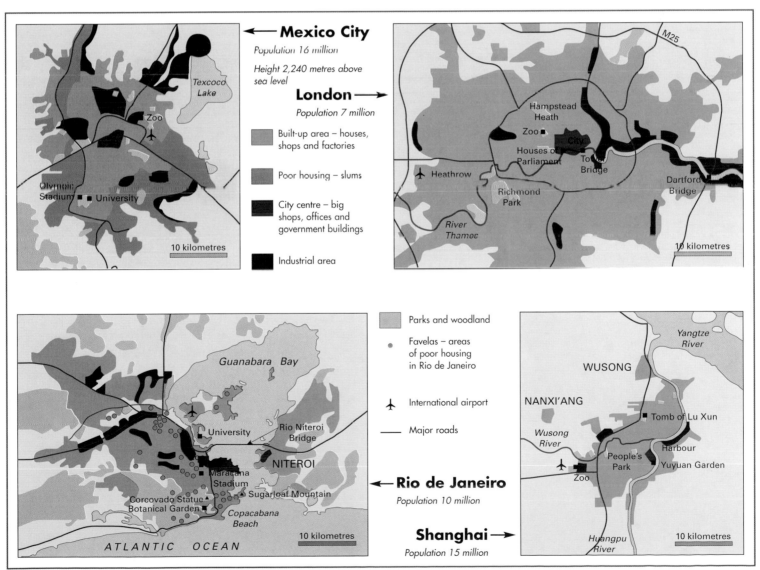

Mexico City ←

Population 16 million

Height 2,240 metres above sea level

London →

Population 7 million

Built-up area – houses, shops and factories

Poor housing – slums

City centre – big shops, offices and government buildings

Industrial area

Parks and woodland

Favelas – areas of poor housing in Rio de Janeiro

✈ International airport

— Major roads

← Rio de Janeiro

Population 10 million

Shanghai →

Population 15 million

World transport

Seaways

— Main shipping routes

■ The biggest seaports in the world (over a hundred million tonnes of cargo handled a year)

● Other big seaports

▨ Ice and icebergs in the sea all the time, or for some part of the year

— Large ships can sail on these rivers

Sea transport is used for goods that are too bulky or heavy to go by air. The main shipping routes are between North America, Europe and the Far East.

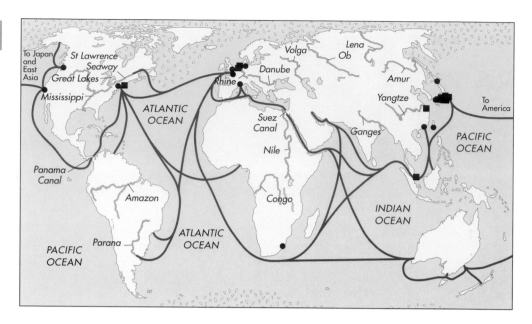

The Panama Canal

Opened in 1914
82 km long
13,000 ships a year

The Suez Canal

Opened in 1870
162 km long
17,000 ships a year

These two important canals cut through narrow pieces of land. Can you work out how much shorter the journeys are by using the canals?

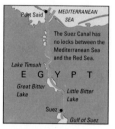

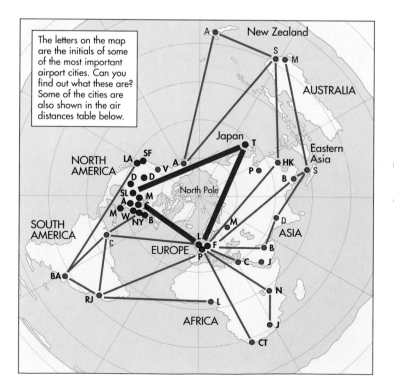

The letters on the map are the initials of some of the most important airport cities. Can you find out what these are? Some of the cities are also shown in the air distances table below.

● Large international airports (over 20 million passengers a year)

● Other important airports

━ Heavily used air routes

─ Other important air routes

Airways

This map has the North Pole at its centre. It shows how much air traffic connects Europe, North America, Japan and Eastern Asia. You can see the long distances in the USA and Russia that are covered by air.

Air distances (kilometres)

	Buenos Aires	Cape Town	London	Los Angeles	New York	Sydney	Tokyo
Buenos Aires		6,880	11,128	9,854	8,526	11,760	18,338
Cape Town	6,880		9,672	16,067	12,551	10,982	14,710
London	11,128	9,672		8,752	5,535	17,005	9,584
Los Angeles	9,854	16,067	8,752		3,968	12,052	8,806
New York	8,526	12,551	5,535	3,968		16,001	10,869
Sydney	11,760	10,982	17,005	12,052	16,001		7,809
Tokyo	18,338	14,710	9,584	8,806	10,869	7,809	

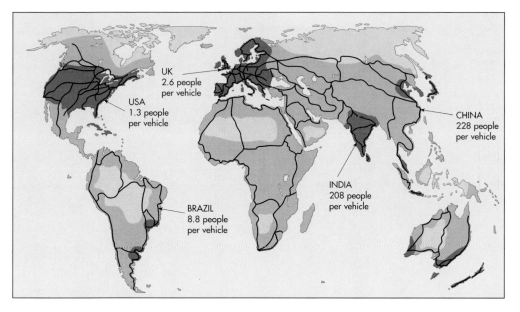

	Many roads and motorways
	Not many roads, few with hard surfaces and many only tracks. Many roads are through-routes.
	No roads or very few roads
——	Important long-distance roads

This map shows some of the major roads that link important cities and ports. It also shows how many people there are in proportion to the number of vehicles in some countries.

UK
2.6 people
per vehicle

USA
1.3 people
per vehicle

CHINA
228 people
per vehicle

INDIA
208 people
per vehicle

BRAZIL
8.8 people
per vehicle

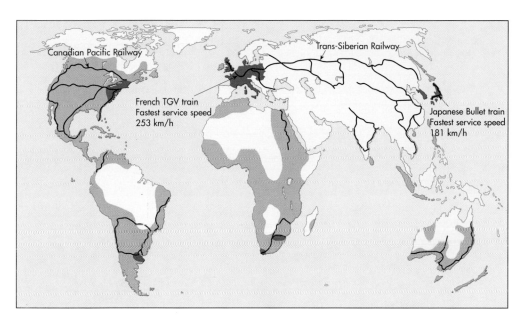

Railways

	Many passenger and goods lines
	Scattered railways often taking goods to and from parts of the coast
	No rail services or very few rail services
——	Important long-distance railways

This map shows some of the important long distance railways in the world. Railways are often used for transporting goods between cities and to ports.

Canadian Pacific Railway

Trans-Siberian Railway

French TGV train
Fastest service speed
253 km/h

Japanese Bullet train
Fastest service speed
181 km/h

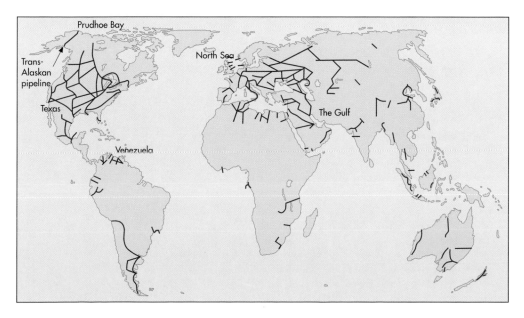

Pipelines

——	Oil and gas pipelines

Pipelines are used for moving oil or gas. Oil and gas are moved to where they will be used or to seaports for loading into tankers to be taken across the sea. The Trans-Alaskan pipeline was built because tankers cannot cross ice. The main oil and gas producing areas of the world are shown on page 39.

Prudhoe Bay

Trans-Alaskan pipeline

Texas

North Sea

The Gulf

Venezuela

Planet in danger

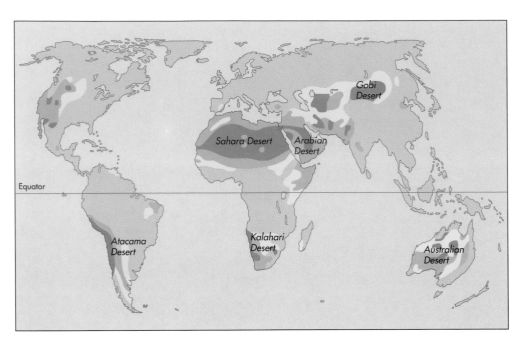

In some parts of the world deserts are expanding. This is because trees are cut down and there are too many animals grazing the land near the desert edge. Soils are not dug properly and they become poorer. Gradually farming becomes impossible and the land becomes desert.

Forests in danger

■ Tropical forests today

■ Tropical forests that have been destroyed or opened up in large areas this century

■ Softwood forests that have suffered damage from air pollution, or cutting down too many trees

The tropical forests are so big that they affect the climate of the whole world. Their area is getting smaller. They are being cut down for wood and to clear land for ranching, 'slash and burn' farming and mining.

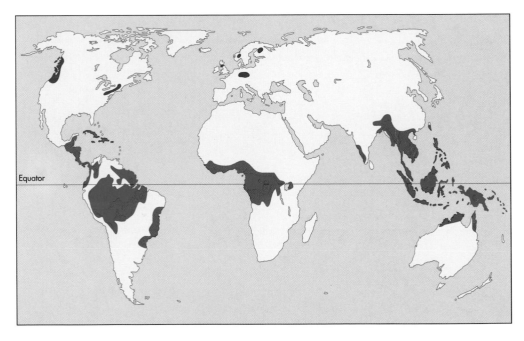

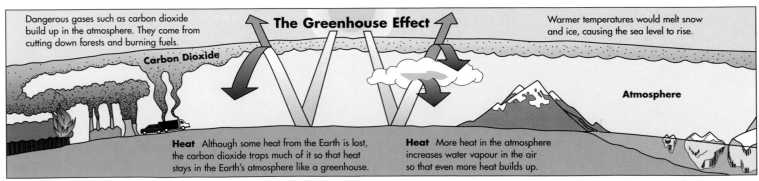

Dangerous gases such as carbon dioxide build up in the atmosphere. They come from cutting down forests and burning fuels.

The Greenhouse Effect

Warmer temperatures would melt snow and ice, causing the sea level to rise.

Carbon Dioxide

Atmosphere

Heat Although some heat from the Earth is lost, the carbon dioxide traps much of it so that heat stays in the Earth's atmosphere like a greenhouse.

Heat More heat in the atmosphere increases water vapour in the air so that even more heat builds up.

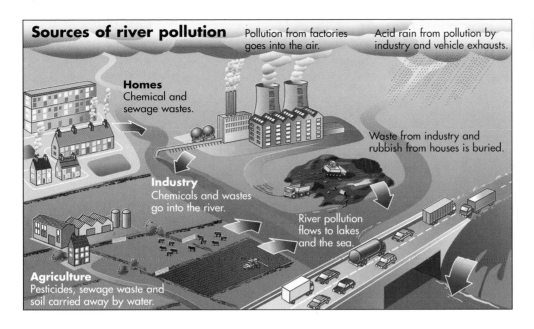

Sources of river pollution

Pollution from factories goes into the air.

Acid rain from pollution by industry and vehicle exhausts.

Homes
Chemical and sewage wastes.

Waste from industry and rubbish from houses is buried.

Industry
Chemicals and wastes go into the river.

River pollution flows to lakes and the sea.

Agriculture
Pesticides, sewage waste and soil carried away by water.

Pollution

This diagram shows some of the ways that we pollute the land, rivers, sea and air around us. Air pollution causes the Earth's atmosphere to become warmer. This is called the 'Greenhouse Effect' (see the diagram at the bottom of the opposite page). The world's climate is gradually changing because of the 'Greenhouse Effect'.

Sea and river pollution

- Bad pollution of the sea and lakes
- Other sea and lake pollution
- Frequent pollution of the sea from oil on shipping routes
- Major oil tanker spills
- Badly polluted rivers

Rubbish and sewage are dumped into the rivers and the sea (see the diagram above). Plants and animals in the water die. Oil tankers sometimes sink and their oil escapes.

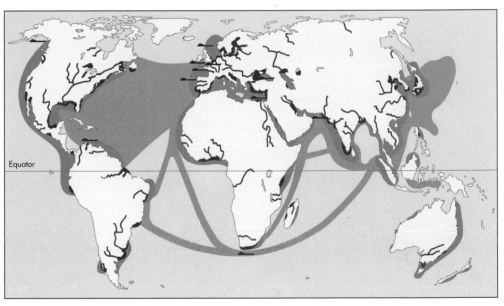

Equator

Air pollution

- Areas where rain can be very acidic
- ■ Large cities that often have unhealthy air

Coal, oil and gas burned in power stations have sulphur and nitrogen in their smoke. This goes into the sky and it combines with rain to make acids (see the diagram on page 21). The acid kills trees and plants, and fish in the rivers and lakes.

Equator

Rich and poor

All countries have both rich and poor people but some countries have more poor people than others. The amount of food that people have to eat and the age that they die can often depend on where they live in the world. The world can be divided into two parts – the North and the South.

The richer countries are in the North and the poorer countries are in the South. The map below shows the dividing line, with Australia and New Zealand in the North. The list on the right shows some contrasts between the North and the South. Some of these contrasts can be seen in the maps on these pages.

North	South
Rich	Poor
Healthy	Poor health
Educated	Poor education
Well fed	Poorly fed
Small families	Large families
Many industries	Few industries
Few farmers	Many farmers
Give aid	Receive aid

The South has over three-quarters of the world's population but less than a quarter of its wealth.

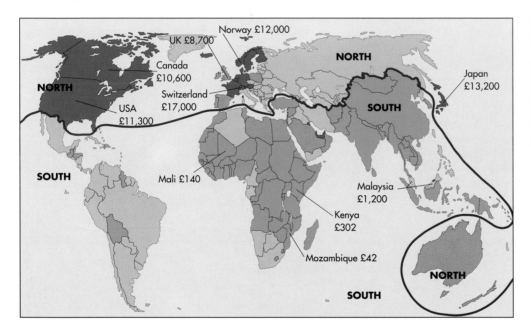

Income

- Very rich countries
- Rich countries
- Poor countries
- Very poor countries

The map shows how much money there is to spend on each person in a country. This is called income per person – this is worked out by dividing the wealth of a country by its population. The map gives examples of rich and poor countries.

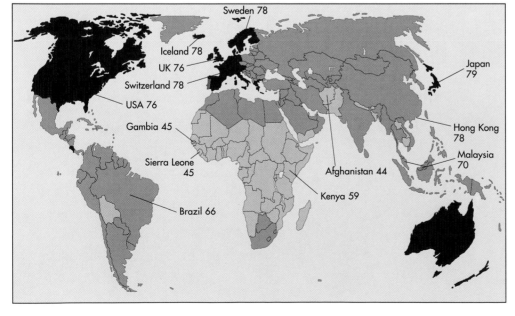

How long do people live?

This is the average age when people die

- Over 75 years
- 60 – 75 years
- Under 60 years

The average age of death is called life expectancy. In the world as a whole, the average life expectancy is 65 years. Some of the highest and lowest ages of death are shown on the map.

Food and famine

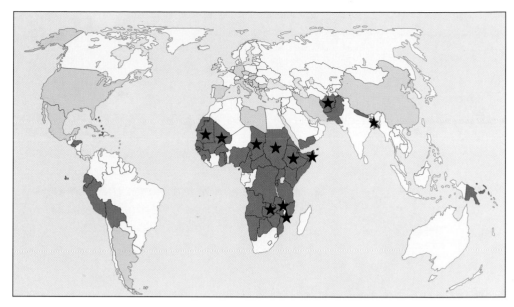

- Below the amount
- Above the amount
- Over a third above the amount

★ Major famines since 1980

If people do not have enough to eat they become unhealthy. This map shows where in the world people have less than and more than the amount of food they need to live a healthy life.

Reading and writing

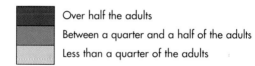

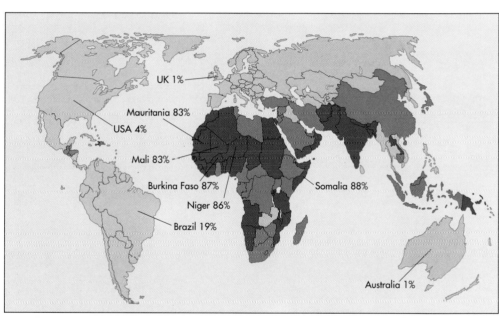

- Over half the adults
- Between a quarter and a half of the adults
- Less than a quarter of the adults

UK 1%
Mauritania 83%
USA 4%
Mali 83%
Burkina Faso 87%
Niger 86%
Brazil 19%
Somalia 88%
Australia 1%

The map shows the proportion of adults in each country who cannot read or write a simple sentence. Can you think of some reasons why more people cannot read or write in some places in the world than in others?

Development aid

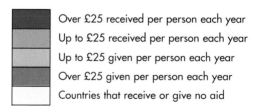

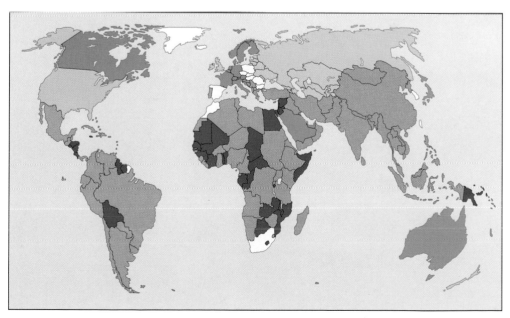

- Over £25 received per person each year
- Up to £25 received per person each year
- Up to £25 given per person each year
- Over £25 given per person each year
- Countries that receive or give no aid

Some countries receive aid from other countries. Money is one type of aid. It is used to help with food, health and education problems. The map shows how much different countries give or receive.

Countries of the World

North America

(see pages 58–59)

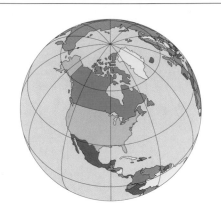

These pages show different maps of the world. The large map shows the world cut through the Pacific Ocean and opened out on to flat paper. The smaller maps of the continents are views of the globe looking down on each of the continents, as they would appear from a spacecraft 32,000 kilometres above the Earth's surface. Larger maps of the continents appear on the following pages. They show more cities than on this map

South America

(see pages 60–61)

Africa

(see pages 54–55)

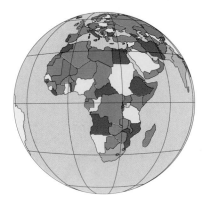

180 160 140 120 100 80

Alaska (U.S.A.)

Arctic Circle

CANADA

UNITED STATES

New York

Los Angeles

Bermuda (U.K.)

ATLA

N O

Tropic of Cancer

BAHAMAS

MEXICO

CUBA

O C

Mexico

Hawaiian Is. (U.S.A.)

JAMAICA HAITI DOM. REP.
ST. KITTS & NEVIS
ANTIGUA & BARBUDA
BELIZE   Puerto   DOMINICA
GUATEMALA   HONDURAS   Rico   ST. LUCIA
                                    (U.S.A.)
EL SALVADOR   ST. VINCENT   BARBADOS
                NICARAGUA   TRINIDAD
                COSTA   & TOBAGO
                RICA   VENEZUELA
                PANAMA
                              GUYANA
                COLOMBIA   SURINAM
                              FRENCH
                              GUIANA

PACIFIC

Kiritimati

Galapagos Is. (Ecuador)   ECUADOR

Equator

Phoenix Islands

KIRIBATI

PERU

BRAZIL

Tokelau Islands (N.Z.)

Marquesas Islands (France)

WESTERN SAMOA   American Samoa (U.S.A.)

FRENCH POLYNESIA   OCEAN

BOLIVIA

Society Islands (France)

Tuamotu Archipelago (France)

Sao Paulo

TONGA   Cook Islands (N.Z.)

Tahiti (France)

Rio Jane

Tubuai Islands (France)

Tropic of Capricorn

Pitcairn Island (U.K.)

Easter Island (Chile)

URUGUAY

Kermadec Islands (N.Z.)

CHILE   ARGENTINA   Buenos Aires

Chatham Islands (N.Z.)

Falkland I (U.K.)

Antarctic Circle

180 160 140 120 100 80

■ All these cities have, or will have by 2000, more than 10 million people

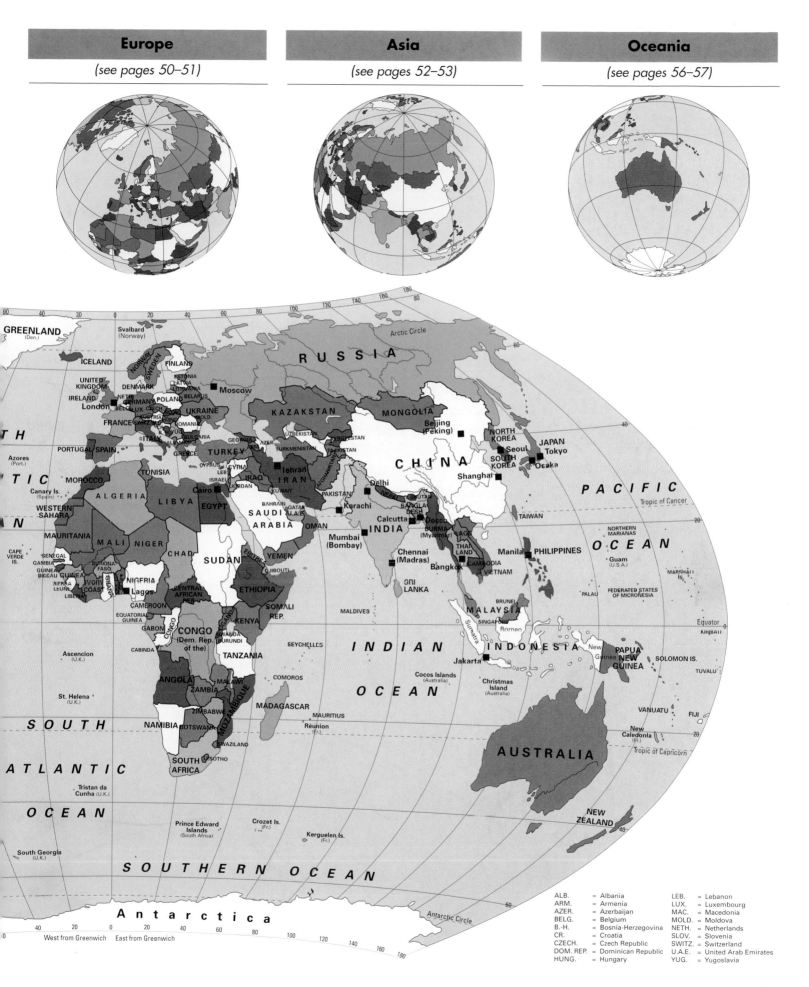

Europe
(see pages 50–51)

Asia
(see pages 52–53)

Oceania
(see pages 56–57)

GREENLAND
(Den.)

Svalbard
(Norway)

Arctic Circle

ICELAND

NORWAY
SWEDEN
FINLAND

R U S S I A

60

UNITED
KINGDOM

DENMARK

ESTONIA
LATVIA
LITHUANIA

Moscow

IRELAND

London

NETH.
GERMANY POLAND
BELG. LUX. CZECH.

BELARUS

FRANCE

AUSTRIA SLOV.

UKRAINE

KAZAKSTAN

MONGOLIA

Beijing
(Peking)

NORTH
KOREA

40

JAPAN

SWITZ. HUNG.
CR. B.-H. ROMANIA
MOLD.

Seoul
Tokyo

ITALY
ALBANIA
BULGARIA

UZBEKISTAN

C H I N A

SOUTH
KOREA

Osaka

PORTUGAL SPAIN

GREECE

TURKEY

GEORGIA

KYRGYZSTAN

Shanghai

P A C I F I C

Azores
(Port.)

CYPRUS

MAC.
YUG.

AZER.

ARM.

TURKMENISTAN

TAJIKISTAN

LEB.
SYRIA

Tehran

AFGHANISTAN

Tropic of Cancer

ISRAEL

IRAQ

I R A N

Canary Is.
(Spain)

MOROCCO

TUNISIA

JORDAN

KUWAIT

PAKISTAN

Delhi

NEPAL
BHUTAN

TAIWAN

O C E A N

20

WESTERN
SAHARA

ALGERIA

LIBYA

Cairo
EGYPT

BAHRAIN QATAR
U.A.E.

SAUDI

Karachi

BANGLA-
DESH

Dacca

NORTHERN
MARIANAS

ARABIA
OMAN

BURMA
(Myanmar)

MAURITANIA

MALI

NIGER

CHAD

SUDAN

YEMEN

Mumbai
(Bombay)

I N D I A

Calcutta

LAOS

Manila

PHILIPPINES

Guam
(U.S.A.)

MARSHALL
IS.

CAPE
VERDE
IS.

SENEGAL
GAMBIA
GUINEA
BISSAU GUINEA

BURKINA
FASO

DJIBOUTI

ERITREA

Chennai
(Madras)

THAI-
LAND

Bangkok

CAMBODIA

VIETNAM

FEDERATED STATES
OF MICRONESIA

PALAU

Equator

SIERRA
LEONE

IVORY
COAST

GHANA

NIGERIA

Lagos

ETHIOPIA

SRI
LANKA

MALDIVES

BRUNEI

MALAYSIA

KIRIBATI

LIBERIA

CAMEROON

CENTRAL
AFRICAN
REP.

SOMALI
REP.

SINGAPORE

Borneo

PAPUA

EQUATORIAL
GUINEA

GABON

CONGO

UGANDA

KENYA

SEYCHELLES

Sumatra

I N D O N E S I A

New
Guinea

NEW
GUINEA

SOLOMON IS.

CONGO
(Dem. Rep.
of the)

RWANDA
BURUNDI

Jakarta

TUVALU

Ascencion
(U.K.)

CABINDA

TANZANIA

I N D I A N

Cocos Islands
(Australia)

ANGOLA

MALAWI

Christmas
Island
(Australia)

VANUATU

FIJI

St. Helena
(U.K.)

ZAMBIA

MOZAMBIQUE

COMOROS

MADAGASCAR

MAURITIUS

O C E A N

ZIMBABWE

Réunion
(Fr.)

New
Caledonia
(Fr.)

20

NAMIBIA

BOTSWANA

SWAZILAND

AUSTRALIA

Tropic of Capricorn

SOUTH
AFRICA

LESOTHO

SOUTH

Tristan da
Cunha (U.K.)

ATLANTIC

O C E A N

NEW
ZEALAND

South Georgia
(U.K.)

Prince Edward
Islands
(South Africa)

Crozet Is.
(Fr.)

Kerguelen Is.
(Fr.)

S O U T H E R N   O C E A N

60

A n t a r c t i c a

Antarctic Circle

West from Greenwich   East from Greenwich

ALB.	= Albania	LEB.	= Lebanon
ARM.	= Armenia	LUX.	= Luxembourg
AZER.	= Azerbaijan	MAC.	= Macedonia
BELG.	= Belgium	MOLD.	= Moldova
B.-H.	= Bosnia-Herzegovina	NETH.	= Netherlands
CR.	= Croatia	SLOV.	= Slovenia
CZECH.	= Czech Republic	SWITZ.	= Switzerland
DOM. REP.	= Dominican Republic	U.A.E.	= United Arab Emirates
HUNG.	= Hungary	YUG.	= Yugoslavia

Europe

Largest countries – by area
(thousand square kilometres)

Russia	17,000
Ukraine	604
France	550
Spain	499

Largest countries – by population
(million people)

Russia	148
Germany	82
United Kingdom	58
Italy	57

Largest cities
(million people)

Paris (FRANCE)	9.5
Moscow (RUSSIA)	9.2
London (UK)	7.0
St Petersburg (RUSSIA)	4.9

- *Europe is the second smallest continent. It is one fifth the size of Asia. Australia is slightly smaller than Europe.*
- *Great Britain is the largest island in Europe. Iceland is the second largest and Ireland is the third largest.*

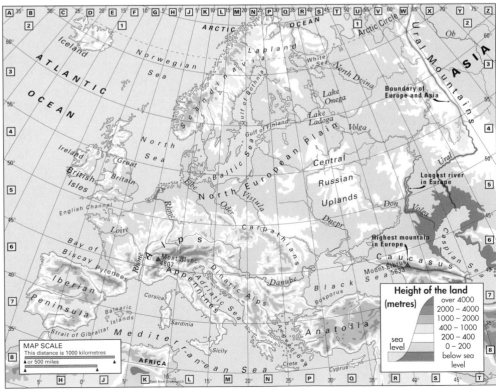

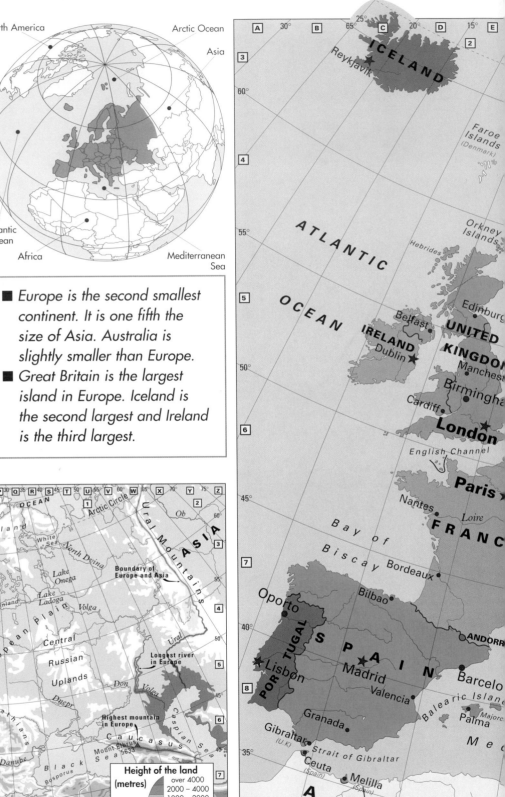

ARCTIC OCEAN

North Cape

Map information

- ■ ● Cities
- ★ Capital city
- ⬜ A Index square - see index
- —— Country boundary
- Sea and lakes

MAP SCALE

This distance is 750 kilometres

or 500 miles

North Cape

Lofoten
Islands

Narvik

Murmansk

White
Sea

Arkhangelsk

North Dvina

Shetland
Islands
(U.K.)

Bergen

Trondheim

Lake Onega

Lake Ladoga

Perm

N O R W A Y

S W E D E N

F I N L A N D

Gulf of Bothnia

Oslo

Stockholm

Helsinki

Gulf of Finland

Tallinn

St. Petersburg

R U S S I A

Volga

Kazan

Moscow

Samara

North
Sea

Gothenburg

ESTONIA

DENMARK

Copenhagen

Riga

LATVIA

LITHUANIA

Baltic Sea

Gdansk

(RUSSIA)

Vilnius

Minsk

BELARUS

Voronezh

NETHERLANDS

Amsterdam

The Hague

Brussels

BELGIUM

GERMANY

LUXEMBOURG

Luxembourg

Frankfurt

Hamburg

Berlin

Elbe

POLAND

Warsaw

Vistula

Krakow

Oder

Kiev

Lvov

Kharkov

U K R A I N E

Volgograd

Don

Volga

Ural

Munich

CZECH
REPUBLIC

Prague

SLOVAK
REPUBLIC

Bratislava

Dnepropetrovsk

Donetsk

Rostov

Caspian Sea

Bern

SWITZERLAND

Rhine

LIECHTENSTEIN

AUSTRIA

Vienna

Budapest

HUNGARY

MOLDOVA

Chisinau

Odessa

Sea of
Azov

Krasnodar

Lyons

Ljubljana

SLOVENIA

Zagreb

CROATIA

ROMANIA

Crimea

Milan

Turin

I T A L Y

MONACO

SAN
MARINO

Adriatic Sea

BOSNIA-
HERZEGOVINA

Sarajevo

YUGOSLAVIA

Belgrade

Bucharest

Danube

Sevastopol

Black Sea

GEORGIA

Tbilisi

AZERBAIJAN

Baku

Marseilles

Corsica
(France)

Rome

BULGARIA

Sofia

Bosporus

ARMENIA

Yerevan

Naples

Sardinia
(Italy)

MACEDONIA

Skopje

Tirane

ALBANIA

Istanbul

Ankara

T U R K E Y

A S I A

Palermo

Sicily

G R E E C E

Aegean Sea

Izmir

Mediterranean Sea

MALTA

Valletta

Athens

Crete

Nicosia

CYPRUS

COPYRIGHT GEORGE PHILIP LTD

51

Asia

Largest countries – by area
(thousand square kilometres)

Russia	17,000
China	9,326
India	2,973

Largest countries – by population
(million people)

China	1,227
India	943
Indonesia	199
Russia	148

Largest cities
(million people)

Tokyo (JAPAN)	26.8
Bombay/Mumbai (INDIA)	15.1
Shanghai (CHINA)	15.1
Beijing (CHINA)	12.4
Calcutta (INDIA)	11.7

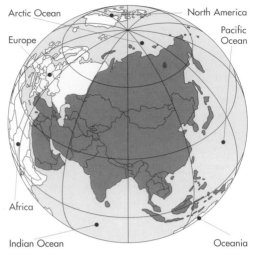

- ■ *Asia is the largest continent. It is twice the size of North America.*
- ■ *It is a continent of long rivers. Many of Asia's rivers are longer than Europe's longest rivers.*
- ■ *Asia contains well over half the world's population.*

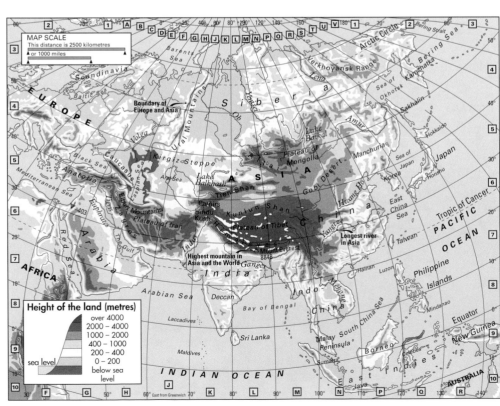

Height of the land (metres)
over 4000 / 2000 – 4000 / 1000 – 2000 / 400 – 1000 / 200 – 400 / 0 – 200 / sea level / below sea level

MAP SCALE
This distance is 2500 kilometres
or 1000 miles

Map information

■● Cities
★ Capital city
A Index square – see index

— Country boundary
▢ Sea and lakes

MAP SCALE
This distance is 2000 kilometres
or 1000 miles

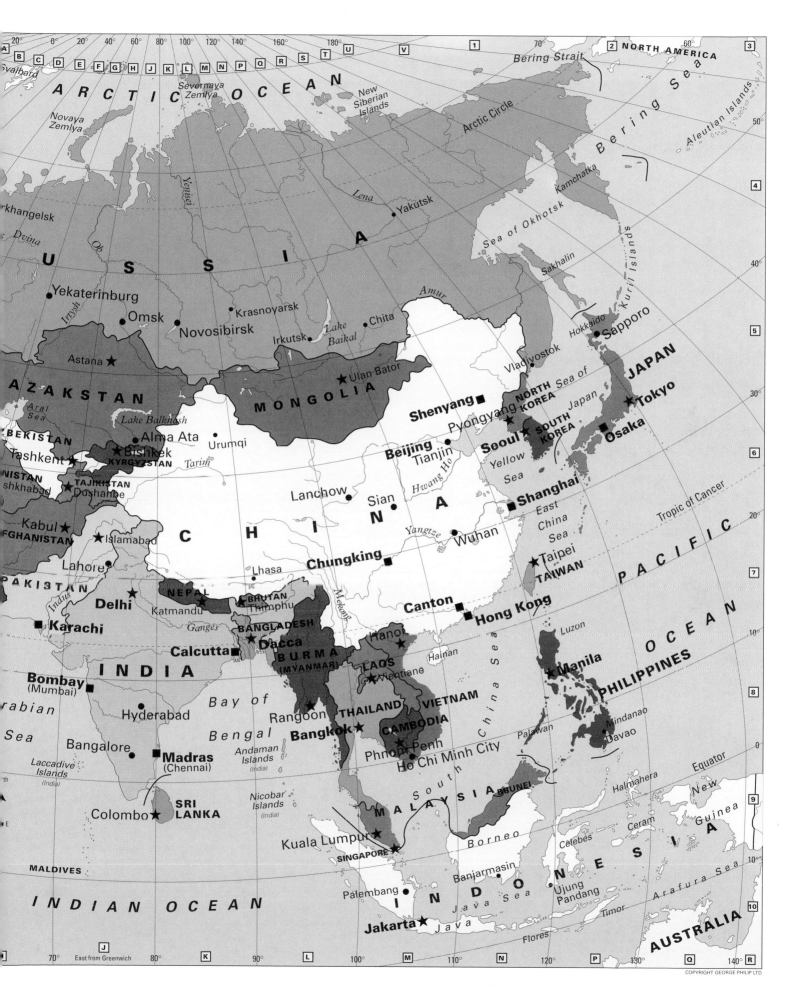

ARCTIC OCEAN

Bering Strait

NORTH AMERICA

Bering Sea

Svalbard

Novaya Zemlya

Severnaya Zemlya

New Siberian Islands

Arctic Circle

Aleutian Islands

Arkhangelsk

Dvina

R U S S I A

Ob

Yenisei

Lena

Yakutsk

Kamchatka

Sea of Okhotsk

Sakhalin

Kuril Islands

Yekaterinburg

Irtysh

Omsk

Novosibirsk

Krasnoyarsk

Irkutsk

Lake Baikal

Chita

Amur

Vladivostok

Hokkaido

Sapporo

Astana

K A Z A K S T A N

Aral Sea

Lake Balkhash

Alma Ata

Urumqi

M O N G O L I A

Ulan Bator

Shenyang ■

Pyongyang ★

NORTH KOREA

Sea of Japan

JAPAN

Tokyo

BEKISTAN

Tashkent ★

Bishkek ★

KYRGYZSTAN

Tarim

Beijing

Tianjin

Seoul ★

SOUTH KOREA

Japan

Osaka

NISTAN

shkabad

TAJIKISTAN

Dushanbe

Yellow Sea

Kabul ★

AFGHANISTAN

Islamabad ★

C H I N A

Lanchow

Sian

Hwang Ho

Shanghai ■

East China Sea

Tropic of Cancer

Lahore

Yangtze

Wuhan

PAKISTAN

Indus

Lhasa

Chungking ■

NEPAL

Katmandu ★

BHUTAN

Thimphu ★

Mekong

Canton ■

Taipei ★

TAIWAN

P A C I F I C

Delhi

Ganges

BANGLADESH

Dacca ★

Hanoi ★

Hong Kong ■

Luzon

O C E A N

Karachi ■

Calcutta ■

BURMA (MYANMAR)

LAOS

Hainan

I N D I A

Bombay (Mumbai) ■

Hyderabad

Bay of

Rangoon ★

THAILAND

Vientiane ★

VIETNAM

Manila ★

PHILIPPINES

rabian

Sea

Bangalore

Bengal

Bangkok ★

CAMBODIA

Phnom Penh ★

Ho Chi Minh City

South

China

Sea

Palawan

Mindanao

Davao

Madras (Chennai) ■

Andaman Islands (India)

Equator

Laccadive Islands (India)

Colombo ★

SRI LANKA

Nicobar Islands (India)

M A L A Y S I A

BRUNEI

Borneo

Halmahera

New

Guinea

Ceram

MALDIVES

Kuala Lumpur ★

SINGAPORE ★

Celebes

Java Sea

Ujung Pandang

Arafura Sea

I N D O N E S I A

I N D I A N   O C E A N

Palembang

Jakarta ★

Java

Timor

Flores

AUSTRALIA

Africa

- Africa is the second largest continent. Asia is the largest.
- There are over 50 countries, some of them small in area and population. The population of Africa is growing more quickly than any other continent.
- Parts of Africa have a dry, desert climate. Other parts are tropical.

- The highest mountains run from north to south on the eastern side of Africa. The Great Rift Valley is a volcanic valley that was formed 10 to 20 million years ago by a crack in the Earth's crust. Mount Kenya and Mount Kilimanjaro are examples of old volcanoes in the area.
- The Sahara desert is the largest desert in the world.

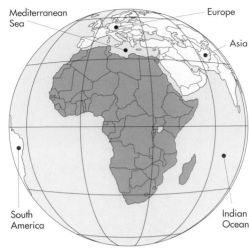

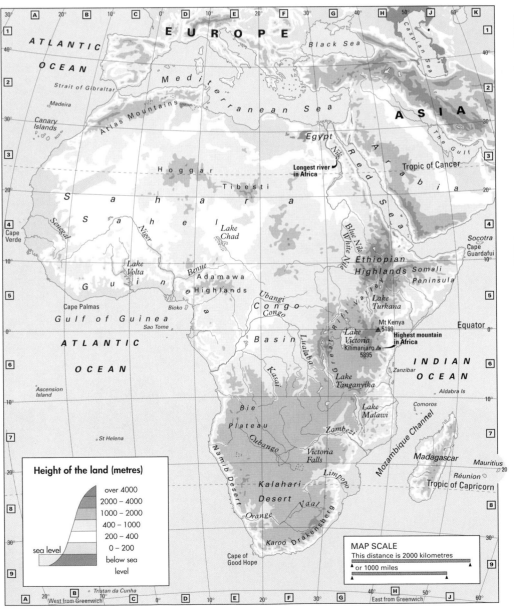

Largest countries – by area

(thousand square kilometres)

Sudan	2,506
Algeria	2,382
Congo (Dem. Rep.)	2,267
Libya	1,760
Niger	1,267
Chad	1,259

Largest countries – by population

(million people)

Nigeria	89
Egypt	64
Ethiopia	52
Congo (Dem. Rep)	45
South Africa	44
Tanzania	30

Largest cities

(million people)

Lagos (NIGERIA)	10.2
Cairo (EGYPT)	9.7
Kinshasa (CONGO, DEM. REP.)	3.8
Alexandria (EGYPT)	3.4
Casablanca (MOROCCO)	2.9

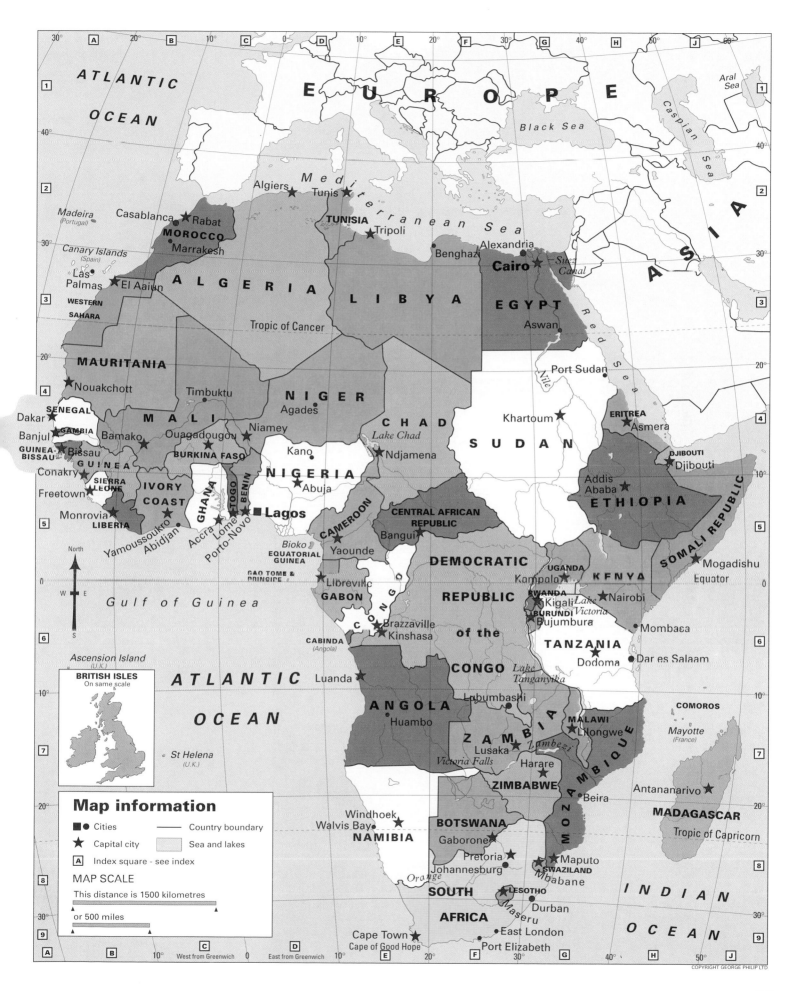

ATLANTIC OCEAN

EUROPE

Aral Sea

Black Sea

Caspian Sea

ASIA

Mediterranean Sea

Madeira *(Portugal)*

Algiers ★ Tunis ★
TUNISIA
Casablanca ● ★ Rabat   Tripoli ★
MOROCCO
● Marrakesh

Canary Islands *(Spain)*

Las ● Palmas
WESTERN SAHARA
El Aaiun ★

Benghazi ●   Alexandria ●
Cairo ★ *Suez Canal*

EGYPT

Aswan ●

Tropic of Cancer

ALGERIA

LIBYA

Red Sea

Port Sudan ●

MAURITANIA

Nouakchott ★

Timbuktu ●

N I G E R

Agades ●

Nile

Khartoum ★
S U D A N

ERITREA
Asmera ★

SENEGAL
Dakar ★
GAMBIA
Banjul ★
Bamako ★
GUINEA-BISSAU
Bissau ★
GUINEA
Conakry ★
SIERRA LEONE
Freetown ★

M A L I

Niamey ★   Kano ●
Ouagadougou ★
BURKINA FASO
NIGERIA
Abuja ★

Lake Chad

C H A D

Ndjamena ★

DJIBOUTI
Djibouti ★

Addis Ababa ★
ETHIOPIA

IVORY COAST
Monrovia ★
LIBERIA

GHANA
Accra ★
TOGO
Lome ★
BENIN
Porto-Novo ★

■ **Lagos**

CAMEROON

Bioko
EQUATORIAL GUINEA
Yaounde ★

CENTRAL AFRICAN REPUBLIC
Bangui ★

SOMALI REPUBLIC

Yamoussoukro ★
Abidjan ●

North

Gulf of Guinea

SAO TOME & PRINCIPE

Libreville ★
GABON

CONGO

DEMOCRATIC REPUBLIC of the CONGO

UGANDA
Kampala ★
RWANDA
Kigali ★
BURUNDI
Bujumbura ★

KENYA
Nairobi ★

Mogadishu ●
Equator

W ——● E
S

Brazzaville ★
CABINDA *(Angola)*
Kinshasa ★

Lake Victoria

Mombasa ●

TANZANIA
Dodoma ★   ● Dar es Salaam

Ascension Island *(U.K.)*

BRITISH ISLES On same scale

ATLANTIC

OCEAN

Luanda ★

Lake Tanganyika

Lubumbashi ●

COMOROS

St Helena *(U.K.)*

ANGOLA
● Huambo

ZAMBIA
Lusaka ★   *Zambezi*
Victoria Falls
MALAWI
Lilongwe ★
Mayotte *(France)*

Harare ★
ZIMBABWE

Beira ●

Antananarivo ★
MADAGASCAR

Tropic of Capricorn

Windhoek ★
Walvis Bay ●
NAMIBIA

BOTSWANA
Gaborone ★

MOZAMBIQUE

Maputo ★
SWAZILAND
Mbabane ★

Pretoria ★ ●
Johannesburg ●
LESOTHO
Maseru ★

Durban ●

INDIAN OCEAN

Orange

SOUTH AFRICA

East London ●

Cape Town ★
Cape of Good Hope
Port Elizabeth ●

Map information

■ ● Cities	—— Country boundary
★ Capital city	▨ Sea and lakes
Ⓐ Index square - see index	

MAP SCALE

This distance is 1500 kilometres

or 500 miles

Australia and Oceania

- The continent is often called Oceania. It is made up of the huge island of Australia and thousands of other islands in the Pacific Ocean.
- It is the smallest continent, only about a sixth the size of Asia.
- The highest mountains are in the islands. Many of them are volcanic.

Largest countries – by area
(thousand square kilometres)

Australia	7,618
Papua New Guinea	453
New Zealand	268

Largest countries – by population
(million people)

Australia	18
Papua New Guinea	4

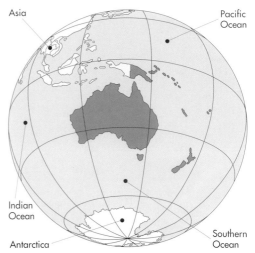

Asia
Pacific Ocean
Indian Ocean
Antarctica
Southern Ocean

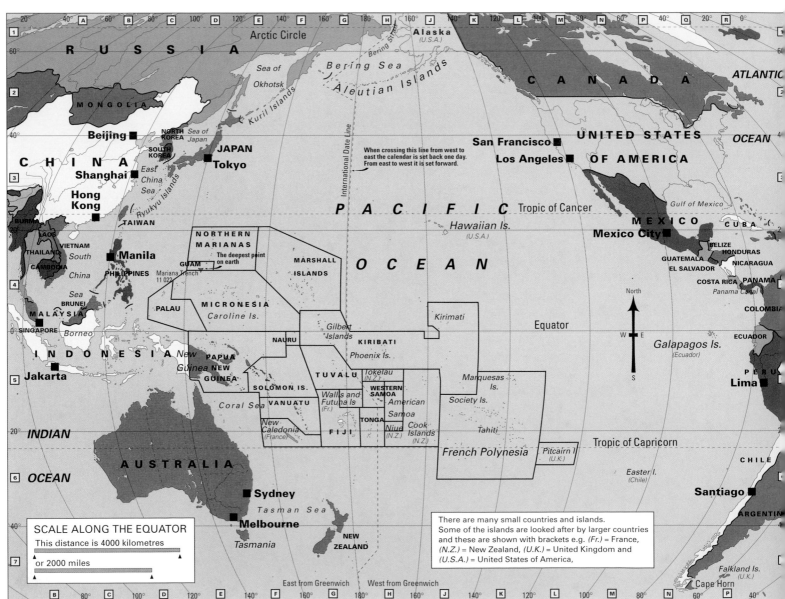

Arctic Circle

RUSSIA

Sea of Okhotsk
Bering Sea
Aleutian Islands
Kuril Islands

Alaska (U.S.A.)

CANADA

ATLANTIC

MONGOLIA

NORTH KOREA Sea of Japan
Beijing
SOUTH KOREA
JAPAN
Tokyo

CHINA
Shanghai
East China Sea

Hong Kong
TAIWAN
Ryukyu Islands

BURMA
LAOS
THAILAND
VIETNAM
CAMBODIA
South China Sea
Manila
PHILIPPINES
BRUNEI
MALAYSIA
SINGAPORE Borneo

INDONESIA

Jakarta

International Date Line

When crossing this line from west to east the calendar is set back one day. From east to west it is set forward.

San Francisco
Los Angeles
UNITED STATES OF AMERICA

OCEAN

PACIFIC

Tropic of Cancer

Hawaiian Is. (U.S.A.)

Gulf of Mexico

MEXICO
CUBA
Mexico City

BELIZE
HONDURAS
GUATEMALA
EL SALVADOR
NICARAGUA
COSTA RICA
PANAMA
Panama Canal

NORTHERN MARIANAS
The deepest point on earth
GUAM
Mariana Trench 11 022

MARSHALL ISLANDS

OCEAN

PALAU
MICRONESIA
Caroline Is.

NAURU
Gilbert Islands
KIRIBATI
Phoenix Is.

Kirimati

Equator

North

COLOMBIA

ECUADOR

Galapagos Is. (Ecuador)

New Guinea
PAPUA NEW GUINEA
SOLOMON IS.

TUVALU
Tokelau (N.Z.)
WESTERN SAMOA
American Samoa

Marquesas Is.
Society Is.

PERU
Lima

VANUATU
Walls and Futuna Is (Fr.)
Coral Sea
Tonga
FIJI
Niue (N.Z.)
Cook Islands (N.Z.)

Tahiti

French Polynesia
Pitcairn I (U.K.)

Tropic of Capricorn

CHILE

INDIAN

New Caledonia (France)

AUSTRALIA

OCEAN

Sydney
Melbourne
Tasman Sea
Tasmania
NEW ZEALAND

Easter I. (Chile)

Santiago

ARGENTINA

SCALE ALONG THE EQUATOR
This distance is 4000 kilometres
or 2000 miles

There are many small countries and islands.
Some of the islands are looked after by larger countries and these are shown with brackets e.g. (Fr.) = France, (N.Z.) = New Zealand, (U.K.) = United Kingdom and (U.S.A.) = United States of America.

East from Greenwich   West from Greenwich

Falkland Is. (U.K.)
Cape Horn

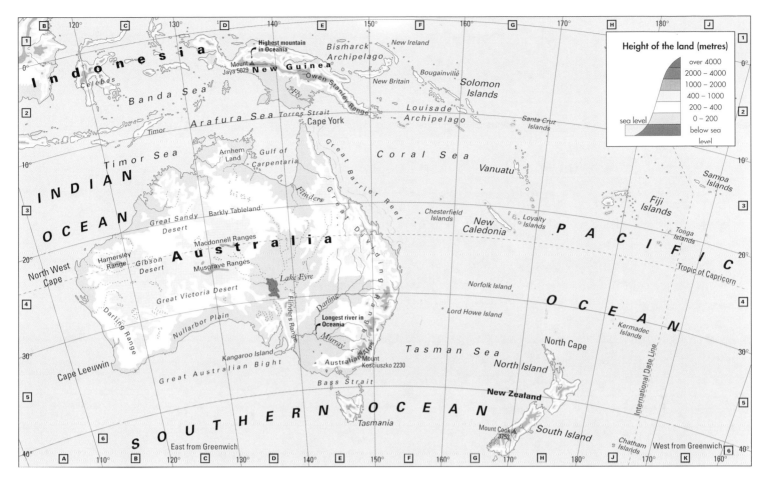

Height of the land (metres)

over 4000
2000 – 4000
1000 – 2000
400 – 1000
200 – 400
0 – 200
below sea level

sea level

First map labels:

Indonesia
Bismarck Archipelago
New Ireland
Highest mountain in Oceania
Mount Jaya 5029
New Guinea
Owen Stanley Range
Bougainville
New Britain
Solomon Islands
Celebes
Banda Sea
Louisade Archipelago
Santa Cruz Islands
Timor
Arafura Sea
Torres Strait
Cape York
Coral Sea
Vanuatu
Samoa Islands
Timor Sea
INDIAN OCEAN
Arnhem Land
Gulf of Carpentaria
Great Barrier Reef
Chesterfield Islands
New Caledonia
Loyalty Islands
Fiji Islands
Tonga Islands
PACIFIC OCEAN
North West Cape
Great Sandy Desert
Barkly Tableland
Macdonnell Ranges
Australia
Hamersley Range
Gibson Desert
Musgrave Ranges
Lake Eyre
Tropic of Capricorn
Darling Range
Great Victoria Desert
Nullarbor Plain
Flinders Range
Longest river in Oceania
Norfolk Island
Lord Howe Island
Kermadec Islands
North Cape
Cape Leeuwin
Great Australian Bight
Kangaroo Island
Murray
Australian Alps
Mount Kosciuszko 2230
Tasman Sea
North Island
New Zealand
International Date Line
Bass Strait
Tasmania
Mount Cook 3753
South Island
Chatham Islands
SOUTHERN OCEAN
East from Greenwich
West from Greenwich

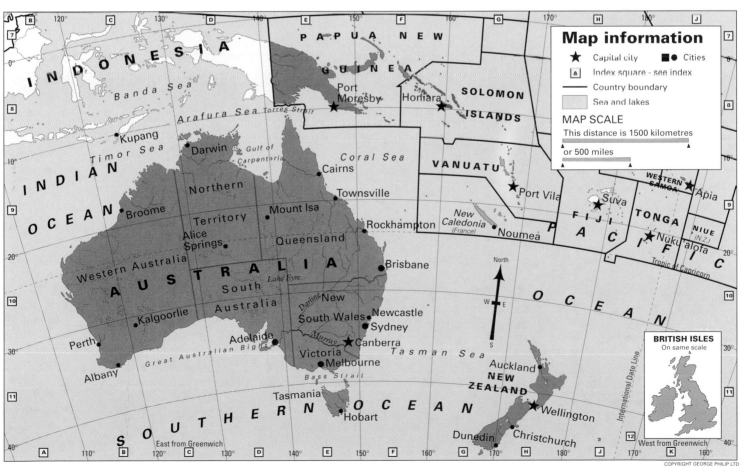

Map information

★ Capital city   ■● Cities

⬛ Index square - see index

— Country boundary

Sea and lakes

MAP SCALE

This distance is 1500 kilometres

or 500 miles

Second map labels:

INDONESIA
PAPUA NEW GUINEA
Port Moresby
Honiara
SOLOMON ISLANDS
Banda Sea
Arafura Sea
Torres Strait
Kupang
Timor Sea
Darwin
Gulf of Carpentaria
Coral Sea
Cairns
VANUATU
WESTERN SAMOA
Apia
INDIAN OCEAN
Broome
Northern Territory
Townsville
Port Vila
Suva
Mount Isa
Rockhampton
New Caledonia (France)
Noumea
FIJI
TONGA
Nuku'alofa
NIUE (N.Z.)
Alice Springs
Queensland
Western Australia
AUSTRALIA
South Australia
Brisbane
Lake Eyre
North
Tropic of Capricorn
PACIFIC OCEAN
Kalgoorlie
Darling
New South Wales
Newcastle
Sydney
Perth
Adelaide
Murray
Canberra
Victoria
Melbourne
Albany
Great Australian Bight
Auckland
Tasman Sea
NEW ZEALAND
Bass Strait
Tasmania
Hobart
Wellington
SOUTHERN OCEAN
Dunedin
Christchurch
East from Greenwich
West from Greenwich
International Date Line

BRITISH ISLES
On same scale

North America

- North America is the third largest continent. It is half the size of Asia. It stretches almost from the Equator to the North Pole.
- Three countries – Canada, the United States and Mexico – make up most of the continent.
- Greenland, the largest island in the world, is included within North America.

- In the east there are a series of large lakes. These are called the Great Lakes. A large waterfall called Niagara Falls is between Lake Erie and Lake Ontario. The St Lawrence river connects the Great Lakes with the Atlantic Ocean.
- There are mountains, volcanoes and high plains in the west, and rivers and lowlands in the east.

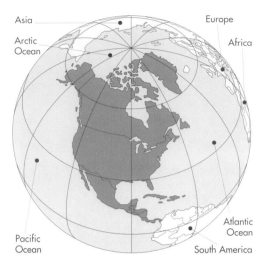

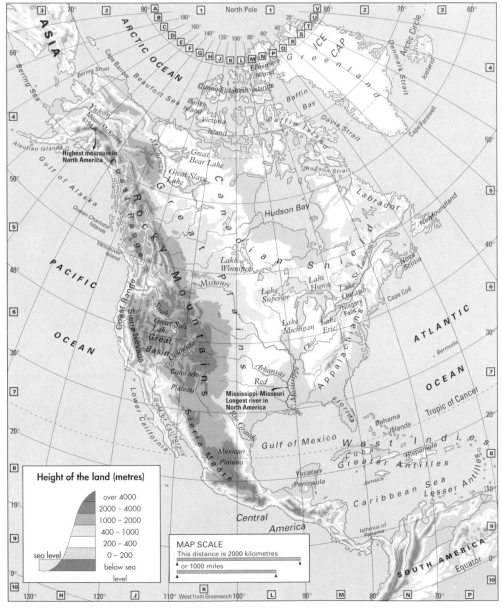

Largest countries – by area

(thousand square kilometres)

Canada 9,221
United States 9,167
Mexico 1,909
Greenland 342
Nicaragua 119
Honduras 112

Largest countries – by population

(million people)

United States 264
Mexico 93
Canada 30
Cuba 11
Guatemala 11
Dominican Republic 8

Largest cities

(million people)

New York (USA) 16.3
Mexico City (MEXICO) 15.6
Los Angeles (USA) 12.4
Chicago (USA) 7.6
Philadelphia (USA) 4.9

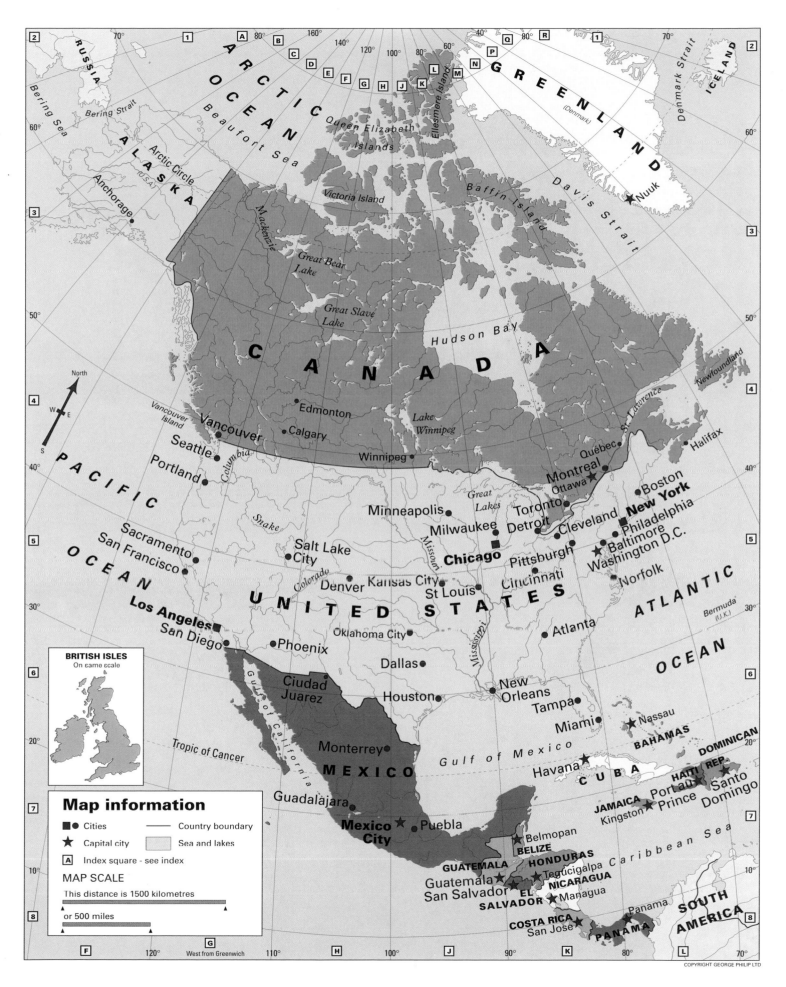

Map information

- ■ ● Cities
- ★ Capital city
- Ⓐ Index square - see index
- —— Country boundary
- Sea and lakes

MAP SCALE

This distance is 1500 kilometres

or 500 miles

BRITISH ISLES
On same scale

ARCTIC OCEAN

RUSSIA

ALASKA (USA)

Bering Sea

Bering Strait

Beaufort Sea

Arctic Circle

Anchorage

Mackenzie

Queen Elizabeth Islands

Ellesmere Island

Victoria Island

Great Bear Lake

Great Slave Lake

Baffin Island

Hudson Bay

GREENLAND (Denmark)

Denmark Strait

ICELAND

Davis Strait

Nuuk

C A N A D A

Newfoundland

Lake Winnipeg

St. Lawrence

PACIFIC OCEAN

North

Vancouver Island

Vancouver

Seattle

Portland

Columbia

Edmonton

Calgary

Winnipeg

Snake

Québec

Halifax

Montreal

Ottawa

Boston

Sacramento

San Francisco

Salt Lake City

Minneapolis

Milwaukee

Detroit

Toronto

Cleveland

New York

Philadelphia

Chicago

Pittsburgh

Baltimore

Washington D.C.

Great Lakes

Missouri

Denver

Kansas City

St Louis

Cincinnati

Norfolk

Colorado

U N I T E D   S T A T E S

ATLANTIC

Los Angeles

San Diego

Phoenix

Oklahoma City

Dallas

Atlanta

Bermuda (U.K.)

OCEAN

Gulf of California

Ciudad Juarez

Houston

New Orleans

Tampa

Mississippi

Miami

Nassau

BAHAMAS

Tropic of Cancer

Monterrey

M E X I C O

Gulf of Mexico

Havana

C U B A

DOMINICAN REP.

HAITI

Santo Domingo

JAMAICA

Port au Prince

Kingston

Guadalajara

Puebla

Mexico City

Belmopan

BELIZE

Caribbean Sea

GUATEMALA

HONDURAS

Tegucigalpa

NICARAGUA

Guatemala

San Salvador

EL SALVADOR

Managua

SOUTH AMERICA

Panama

COSTA RICA

San Jose

PANAMA

West from Greenwich

COPYRIGHT GEORGE PHILIP LTD

59

South America

- The Amazon is the second longest river in the world. The Nile is the longest river, but more water flows from the Amazon into the ocean than from any other river.
- The range of mountains called the Andes runs for over 7,500 km from north to south on the western side of the continent. There are many volcanoes in the Andes.
- Lake Titicaca is the largest lake in the continent. It has an area of 8,200 sq km and is 3,800 metres above sea level.
- Spanish and Portuguese are the principal languages spoken in South America.
- Brazil is the largest country in area and population and is the richest in the continent.

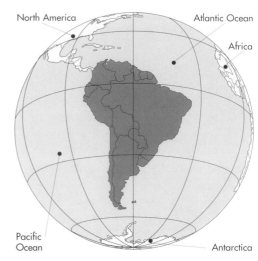

MAP SCALE
This distance is 2000 kilometres
or 1000 miles

Height of the land (metres)

over 4000
2000 – 4000
1000 – 2000
400 – 1000
200 – 400
0 – 200
below sea level
sea level

Largest countries – by area

(thousand square kilometres)

Brazil	8,457
Argentina	2,737
Peru	1,208
Bolivia	1,084
Colombia	1,039
Venezuela	882

Largest countries – by population

(million people)

Brazil	161
Colombia	35
Argentina	35
Peru	24
Venezuela	22
Chile	14

Largest cities

(million people)

Sao Paulo (BRAZIL)	16.4
Buenos Aires (ARGENTINA)	11.0
Rio de Janeiro (BRAZIL)	9.9
Lima (PERU)	6.6
Bogota (COLOMBIA)	5.0

B	90°	C	80°	D	70°	E	60°	F	50°	G	40°	H

1

Havana
CUBA
BAHAMAS
DOMINICAN REP.
HAITI
PUERTO RICO (U.S.A.)
VIRGIN IS. (U.S.A.-U.K.)
ST KITTS-NEVIS
ANTIGUA & BARBUDA

20°

MEXICO
JAMAICA
Port au Prince
Santo Domingo
GUADELOUPE (France)
DOMINICA
MARTINIQUE (France)
ST LUCIA
BARBADOS

BELIZE
Kingston

ATLANTIC

2

GUATEMALA
HONDURAS
Tegucigalpa
NICARAGUA
EL SALVADOR
Managua

Caribbean Sea
NETHERLANDS ANTILLES
ST VINCENT
GRENADA

OCEAN

Barranquilla
Caracas
Port of Spain
TRINIDAD & TOBAGO

10°

COSTA RICA
Panama Canal
Maracaibo
Valencia
Orinoco

San Jose
Panama
PANAMA
VENEZUELA
Georgetown
Paramaribo
Cayenne

3

Medellin
Bogota
GUYANA
SURINAM
FRENCH GUIANA

COLOMBIA
Cali

Quito
ECUADOR
Negro
Amazon
Belem
Equator

0°

Galapagos Islands (Ecuador)
Guayaquil
Iquitos
Manaus
Fortaleza

4

Chiclayo
Madeira
Tapajos

Trujillo
B R A Z I L
Ucayali
Xingu
Tocantins
Recife

PERU
Sao Francisco

10°

Lima
Cuzco
Salvador

Arequipa
Lake Titicaca
Brasilia

5

La Paz
Goiania

BOLIVIA
Sucre
Belo Horizonte

20°

Antofagasta
PARAGUAY
Parana
Sao Paulo
Rio de Janeiro

6

Asuncion
Curitiba
Tropic of Capricorn

CHILE
ATLANTIC

Tucuman
Porto Alegre

Cordoba
URUGUAY

30°

Valparaiso
Rosario
Montevideo

Santiago
Buenos Aires
Rio de la Plata
OCEAN

Concepcion
ARGENTINA

7

North
W E
S

BRITISH ISLES
On same scale

Bahia Blanca

Map information

■ Cities   — Country boundary
★ Capital city   Sea and lakes
A Index square - see index

MAP SCALE
This distance is 1500 kilometres
or 500 miles

40°

8

Falkland Islands (U.K.)
Stanley

South Georgia (U.K.)

Punta Arenas
Cape Horn

PACIFIC OCEAN

50°

Juan Fernandez (Chile)

COPYRIGHT GEORGE PHILIP LTD

50°	A	100°	B	90°	C	80°	D	70°	E	60°	F	50°	G	40°	H	30°	J	20°

9

Polar Regions

The Polar Regions are the areas around the North Pole and the South Pole. The area around the North Pole is called the **Arctic** and the area around the South Pole is called the **Antarctic**. The sun never shines straight down on the Arctic or Antarctic so they are very cold – the coldest places on Earth. The Arctic consists of frozen water. Some parts of Northern Europe, North America and Asia are inside the Arctic Circle. A group of people called the Inuit live there.

Map information

- Cities and towns
★ Capital cities
● (Japan)
Scientific stations in the Antarctic

Cross-section

Land covered in ice

Ice always in the sea

Ice sometimes in the sea

MAP SCALE
This distance is 1500 kilometres

or 500 miles

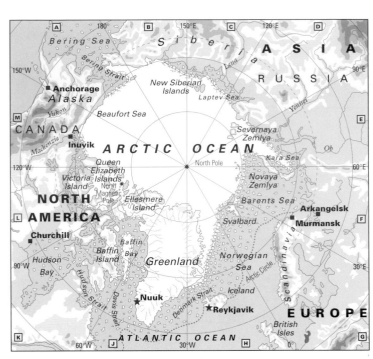

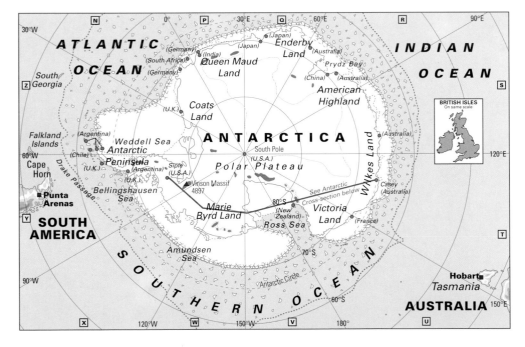

The Antarctic is a continent. It is bigger than Europe or Australia. There is no permanent population. Most of the land consists of ice which is thousands of metres thick. At the edges, chunks of ice break off to make icebergs. These float out to sea. The diagram below shows a cross-section through Antarctica between two of the scientific research stations, Siple and Casey. It shows how thick the ice is on the ice sheets.

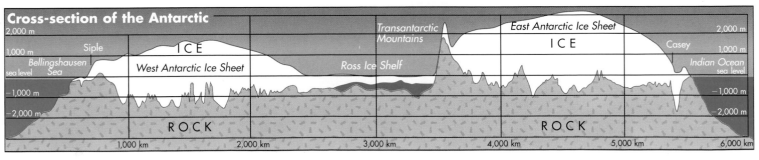

Cross-section of the Antarctic

— UK, Europe and the World —

The UN is the largest international organization in the world. The headquarters are in New York and 185 countries are members. It was formed in 1945 to help solve world problems and to help keep world peace. The UN sends peacekeeping forces to areas where there are problems.

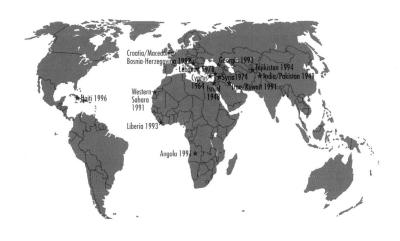

★ Peacekeeping forces with the year they were sent

European Union

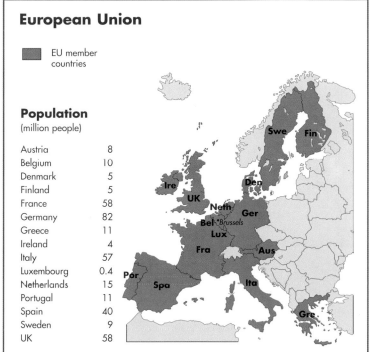

■ EU member countries

Population
(million people)

Austria	8
Belgium	10
Denmark	5
Finland	5
France	58
Germany	82
Greece	11
Ireland	4
Italy	57
Luxembourg	0.4
Netherlands	15
Portugal	11
Spain	40
Sweden	9
UK	58

The EU was first formed in 1951. Six countries were members. Now there are 15 countries in the EU. These countries meet to discuss agriculture, industry and trade as well as social and political issues. The headquarters are in Brussels. The total population of the countries in the EU is over 340 million, more than Japan (125 million) and the USA (264 million).

The Commonwealth

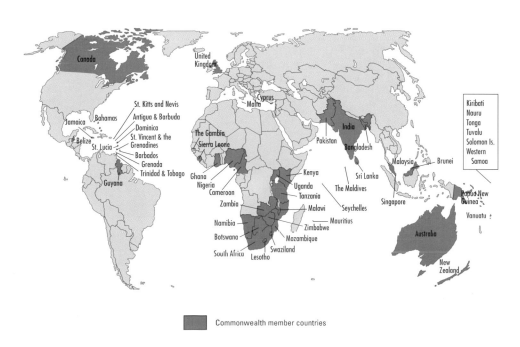

■ Commonwealth member countries

The Commonwealth is a group of 53 independent countries which used to belong to the British Empire. It is organized by a group of people called the Secretariat which is based in London. Queen Elizabeth II is the head of the Commonwealth. About every two years the heads of the different governments meet to discuss world problems. These meetings are held in different countries in the Commonwealth.

Index